KW-326-441

Volker Wieland
Editor

# THE SCIENCE AND PRACTICE OF MONETARY POLICY TODAY

## THE DEUTSCHE BANK PRIZE IN FINANCIAL ECONOMICS 2007

 Springer

*Editor*
Prof. Dr. Volker Wieland
Center for Financial Studies
House of Finance
Grüneburgplatz 1
60323 Frankfurt am Main
Germany
wieland@ifk-cfs.de

and

Goethe University Frankfurt
Department of Economics and Business Administration
Grüneburgplatz 1
60323 Frankfurt am Main
wieland@wiwi.uni-frankfurt.de

ISBN 978-3-642-02952-3                    e-ISBN 978-3-642-02953-0
DOI 10.1007/978-3-642-02953-0
Springer Heidelberg Dordrecht London New York

Library of Congress Control Number: 2009940799

© Springer-Verlag Berlin Heidelberg 2010
This work is subject to copyright. All rights are reserved, whether the whole or part of the material is concerned, specifically the rights of translation, reprinting, reuse of illustrations, recitation, broadcasting, reproduction on microfilm or in any other way, and storage in data banks. Duplication of this publication or parts thereof is permitted only under the provisions of the German Copyright Law of September 9, 1965, in its current version, and permission for use must always be obtained from Springer. Violations are liable to prosecution under the German Copyright Law.
The use of general descriptive names, registered names, trademarks, etc. in this publication does not imply, even in the absence of a specific statement, that such names are exempt from the relevant protective laws and regulations and therefore free for general use.

*Cover design:* WMXDesign GmbH, Heidelberg, Germany

Printed on acid-free paper

Springer is part of Springer Science+Business Media (www.springer.com)

# EDITOR'S FOREWORD

This book presents important aspects of the New-Keynesian theory of monetary policy and its implications for the practical decision making of central bankers today. It brings together several new research contributions that were presented at the scientific symposium on the occasion of the award of the Deutsche Bank Prize in Financial Economics 2007 to Professor Michael Woodford of Columbia University. Woodford received this prize according to the jury in recognition of his fundamental contributions to the theory and practical analysis of monetary policy. The prize jury included Günter Franke, Michael Haliassos, Otmar Issing, Jan Krahnen, Patrick Lane, Lucrezia Reichlin, Reinhardt Schmidt, Lars Svensson, Norbert Walter and Volker Wieland.

The first part on "The New-Keynesian Approach to Understanding the Economy" contains two chapters written by Bennett McCallum and Jordi Galí, respectively. McCallum provides an exposition of key elements of the New-Keynesian approach to monetary policy analysis and an appreciation of Woodford's contributions. Galí further develops several key lessons of this approach and points out important new directions for further research.

The second part on "The New-Keynesian Approach in Forecasting and Monetary Policy Design" contains three chapters that build bridges between the theory and practice of monetary policy. Michael Woodford draws out the policy conclusions of the New-Keynesian approach and presents his case for forecast targeting as a strategy for the practical conduct of monetary policy. Domenico Giannone, Francesca Monti and Lucrezia Reichlin then show how to combine forecasts from quarterly macroeconomic models of the New-Keynesian variety with additional timely information that is available at a monthly frequency. Guenter Beck and Volker Wieland address recent criticisms that the New-Keynesian approach fails to explain money and inflation trends. They point to central bank misperceptions regarding potential output as a root cause of such trends and show that monetary aggregates can serve as a useful cross-check to a forecast targeting strategy.

In the third part Frederic Mishkin goes on to address the question "Will monetary policy become more of a science?" Mishkin, who served as a Governor at the Board of Governors of the Federal Reserve System when he wrote this chapter, provides new insights from a theoretical as well as a practical perspective as central bank decision maker.

The final part reports on the scientific symposium in honor of Michael Woodford. It includes statements by Josef Ackermann, Volker Wieland and Hermann-Josef Lamberti as well as a detailed summary of the symposium written by Celia Wieland. In conclusion, a panel discussion with Norbert Walter, Stefan Gerlach, Patrick Lane and Otmar Issing offers new insights regarding the New-Keynesian approach, its successes, failures and some important open questions.

Volker Wieland
(Goethe University Frankfurt and CFS)

# TABLE OF CONTENTS

## THE DEUTSCHE BANK PRIZE
## IN FINANCIAL ECONOMICS 2007:
## AWARD CEREMONY
## AND SCIENTIFIC SYMPOSIUM
## IN HONOR OF MICHAEL WOODFORD

## THE THEORY AND PRACTICE
## OF MONETARY POLICY TODAY –
## SUCCESSES, FAILURES AND OPEN QUESTIONS

# LIST OF AUTHORS

Volker Wieland
Department of Economics and Business
Administration
Goethe University Frankfurt
Grüneburgplatz 1
60323 Frankfurt am Main
Germany
E-Mail: wieland@wiwi.uni-frankfurt.de

Bennet T. McCallum
Tepper School of Business
Carnegie Mellon University
5000 Forbes Avenue
Pittsburgh, PA 15213
U.S.A.
E-Mail : bmccallum@cmu.edu

Jordi Galí
Department of Economics and Business
Universitat Pompeu Fabra
Jaume I Building
Ramon Trias Fargas, 25-27
08005 Barcelona
Spain
E-Mail: jgali@crei.cat

Michael Woodford
Department of Economics
Columbia University
420 W. 118th Street
New York, NY 10027
U.S.A.
E-Mail: michael.woodford@columbia.edu

Domenico Giannone
European Central Bank
Kaiserstrasse 29
60311 Frankfurt am Main
Germany
E-Mail: dgiannon@ulb.ac.be

Francesca Monti
ECARES Université Libre de Bruxelles
50, avenue Roosevelt  CP 114
1050 Bruxelles
Belgium
E-Mail: fmonti@ulb.ac.be

Lucrezia Reichlin
London Business School
Regent's Park
London
NW1 4SA
United Kingdom
E-Mail: lreichlin@london.edu

Günter Beck
Department of Economics and Business
Administration
Goethe University Frankfurt
Grüneburgplatz 1
60323 Frankfurt am Main
Germany
E-Mail: gbeck@wiwi.uni-frankfurt.de

Frederic S. Mishkin
Columbia Business School
3022 Broadway, Uris Hall 817
New York, NY 10027
U.S.A.
E-Mail: fsm3@columbia.edu

Josef Ackermann
Deutsche Bank AG
Theodor-Heuss-Allee 70
60486 Frankfurt am Main
Germany

Hermann-Josef Lamberti
Deutsche Bank AG
Theodor-Heuss-Allee 70
60486 Frankfurt am Main
Germany

Celia Wieland
wieland EconConsult
Lichtensteinstr. 6
60322 Frankfurt am Main
Germany
E-Mail: info@wieland-econconsult.com

Norbert Walter
Deutsche Bank AG
Theodor-Heuss-Allee 70
60486 Frankfurt am Main
Germany
E-Mail: norbert.walter@db.com

Stefan Gerlach
Institute for Monetary and Financial Stability
House of Finance
Goethe University Frankfurt
Grüneburgplatz 1, HPF H12
60323 Frankfurt am Main
Germany
E-Mail: stefan.gerlach@wiwi.uni-frankfurt.de

Patrick Lane
The Economist
25 St James's Street
London SW1A 1HG
United Kingdom
E-Mail: patricklane@economist.com

Otmar Issing
Center for Financial Studies
House of Finance
Goethe University Frankfurt
Grüneburgplatz 1, HPF H5
60323 Frankfurt am Main
Germany
E-Mail: issing@ifk-cfs.de

# THE NEW-KEYNESIAN
# APPROACH TO
# UNDERSTANDING
# THE ECONOMY

# MICHAEL WOODFORD'S CONTRIBUTIONS TO MONETARY ECONOMICS*

Bennett T. McCallum (Carnegie Mellon University)

## Introduction

Michael Woodford has contributed so much important and path-breaking research that it would be impossible to cover all of it in this talk. Also, I have had a difficult time knowing whether to speak about his contributions or about the New-Keynesian approach more generally. So I will start with neither of these and instead try to tell a bit about Woodford as a person, but from a professional perspective. I believe that I first met him in 1985 at a research conference in Austin, Texas, where we were both presenting papers on monetary economics conducted in overlapping genera-tion (OG) models. I was, at the time, having arguments with some economists who had been deriving several startling results in OG models, basically because their setups gave "money" no medium-of-exchange properties – it provided no transaction-facilitating services to its hold-ers. It also paid no interest, so if the model economy included capital or land no one would want to hold *any* money unless prices were fall-ing rapidly enough. I thought that this was a foolish approach, but was very nervous about making the argument because these other econ-omists were quite prominent – and I feared that Michael would support their position. Well, it turned out that his model did give money a medium-of-exchange role, so that was fine with me.[1] That was my first indication that Wood-ford rarely (if ever) does anything that is truly foolish.

The next time we met was later in 1985 when he was visiting Carnegie Mellon for a few months. I had not actually seen him until he came to my office one day to tell me, very politely, that a published argument of mine concerning rational expectations (RE) solu-tion multiplicity was incorrect. His explanation (Woodford, 1990) was beyond my understand-ing. I think that I understand it somewhat better now, since we have been having various closely related differences ever since. He has, of course, been winning the arguments. Thus, I have been converted to (approximately) his position that the criterion of *learnability* — E-stability in the Evans-Honkapohja (2001) approach – is funda-mental to the plausibility of a RE equilibrium.

* Paper prepared for presentation at the Center for Financial Studies academic symposium, "The Theory and Practice of Monetary Policy Today," in honor of Professor Michael Woodford, recipient of the Deutsche Bank Prize in Financial Economics 2007 (held at Frankfurt University on October 4, 2007). I am indebted to Marvin Goodfriend for helpful comments.

[1] Our conference papers were Woodford (1985) and McCallum (1985).

A second disagreement nicely illustrates Woodford's collegiality as well as his analytical mastery. It concerns the "fiscal theory of the price level" (FTPL), of which he has been one of the main proponents. He gave an important paper on the topic at the Carnegie-Rochester conference of November 1994, stressing aspects of the theory that would be upsetting to Allan Meltzer, myself, and others present.[2] It generated a lot of interest among a variety of economists. Meltzer and I were doubtful and could not understand, despite much effort, what the crucial differences were. A few months later, I met Michael at a conference in San Francisco and tried to explain my puzzlement to him. The next morning he handed me one sheet of paper that, by focusing on a particular solution to a carefully chosen example, got to the core of the issue clearly and dramatically. Since then, I have used his example in writings that argue against the FTPL.[3] He continues to disagree with me and other critics but in his outstanding treatise, *Interest and Prices*, he mentions the FTPL only briefly and does not use it in developing the main analysis. That shows great common-sense judgment, another of his characteristics.

These examples suggest that he and I have had professional disputes over the years. That is true; I feel that I've spent much of my time over the past decade arguing with positions of his. Does that make me an inappropriate person to discuss his work at this occasion? I don't think so; I would say that it makes my admiration of him as an analyst and as a person all the more meaningful.

## Interest and Prices

What should one say about Woodford's (2003) book, *Interest and Prices*? At a conference in 2000 I suggested that he was trying to improve on Don Patinkin's (1956) classic work *Money, Interest, and Prices* by "taking out the 'money'." That was an attempt at a joke, because in fact Woodford's book does drastically diminish the role of money in monetary policy analysis. But despite that, my evaluation is that this book is the most important treatise on monetary economics in over 50 years; it seems likely to go down in intellectual history as one of the handful of great books on this topic. It features an enormous amount of detailed analysis, designed to provide a rigorous theoretical foundation for today's mainstream approach, together with concern for empirical regularities in actual data and also well-written explanations of strategic aspects of the approach. It has become the bible for a generation of young scholars who will likely dominate monetary economics for the next couple of decades.

## The New-Keynesian Approach

How does *Interest and Prices* relate to the New-Keynesian approach mentioned in our program for today? Well, it is the most important example of today's mainstream approach, which is often referred to as "New-Keynesian."[4] I do not particularly like that term, myself, because the approach has as much reason to be called "New-Neoclassical-Synthesis," as it was by Goodfriend and King (1997). In fact, in some important respects the approach is actually closer to that of the "monetarists" of the 1960s and '70s than the "Keynesians" who they battled with. In that regard, I have in mind its emphasis on monetary policy rules, individual optimization, low inflation, and non-exploitation of output-inflation trade-offs.

For non-specialists it may be helpful to write down a very small system of equations that is representative of the basic model used in

---

[2] Woodford (1995).
[3] McCallum (2003).
[4] An early and influential example is Clarida, Gali, and Gertler (1999).

*Interest and Prices* and in current New-Keynesian (NK) analysis more generally. Consider the following simple three-equation system:

$$y_t = b_0 + E_t y_{t+1} + b_1 (R_t - E_t \Delta p_{t+1}),$$
$$b_2 (g_t - E_t g_{t+1}) + v_t, \quad b_1 < 0, \, b_2 > 0, \qquad (1)$$

$$\Delta p_t = E_t \Delta p_{t+1} + \kappa (y_t - \bar{y}_t) + u_t, \quad \kappa > 0, \quad (2)$$

$$R_t = \mu_0 + \Delta p_1 + \mu_1 (\Delta p_t - \Delta p^*) +$$
$$\mu_2 (y_t - \bar{y}_t) + e_t, \quad \mu_1 > 0, \, \mu_2 \geq 0. \qquad (3)$$

Here equations (1)-(3) represent an expectational IS equation, a price-adjustment relationship, and a Taylor-style monetary policy rule, respectively. The basic variables are $y_t$ = log of output, $p_t$ = log of price level, and $R_t$ = nominal one-period interest rate, so $\Delta p_t$ represents inflation, $R_t - E_t \Delta p_{t+1}$ is the real interest rate, and $y_t - \bar{y}_t \equiv \tilde{y}_t$ is the fractional output gap (output relative to its capacity or natural rate value, whose log is $\bar{y}_t$).

Also, $g_t$ represents the log of government purchases, which for present purposes we take to be exogenous. In this system, $E_t$ denotes the expectations operator conditional on information available at time t, so $E_t \Delta p_{t+1}$ is the rational expectation formed at time t of $\Delta p_{t+1}$, the inflation rate one period in the future. In his book, Woodford painstakingly shows that (1) and (2) can be derived from optimizing behavior on the part of households and producers, respectively, under plausible simplifying assumptions (and using some carefully justified approximations).

Note that no variable labeled $m_t$, representing a monetary aggregate, appears anywhere in this model. We could add:

$$m_t - p_t = \gamma_0 + \gamma_1 y_t + \gamma_2 R_t + \eta_t, \quad \gamma_1 > 0, \, \gamma_2 < 0, \quad (4)$$

a traditional money demand equation that would be consistent with the optimizing analysis. But its specification would not affect the processes generating $y_t$, $p_t$ and $R_t$ – if the central bank is managing policy as in (3). Then (4) would just determine how much money has to be supplied to make (3) consistent with money demand. Thus (4) can be ignored by the central bank and by analysts-and usually is ignored in NK analysis.

In principle, a central bank can manage monetary policy either way, but in fact most use procedures like (3). Woodford (2007) argues, against the official position of the European Central Bank, that nothing useful is lost by ignoring the behavior of $m_t$. Although I am sympathetic to the opposing point of view, it appears to me that Michael is at present winning this dispute.

Given that use of some $R_t$ policy rule analogous to (3) is a distinguishing characteristic of NK analysis, I must mention that this practice got a tremendous boost from the famous 1993 paper by John Taylor, in which (3) with $\mu_1 = 1/2$, $\mu_2 = 1/2$, $\Delta p^* = 2$, $\mu_0 = 2$ was proposed. Taylor's paper was doubly fruitful, as it encouraged academic researchers to think of policy as being implemented by interest rates and simultaneously encouraged central bank economists to think in terms of policy *rules* – i.e., systematic patterns of behavior – while also showing that the effective Federal Reserve policy over 1987-1992 was quite well-described by rule (3). This had the effect of bringing central bank and academic research much closer together, to the point that now one cannot distinguish between them.

In *Interest and Prices*, Woodford develops in detail the fact that (1) and (2) reflect optimizing behavior for the economy's private agents (under simplifying but plausible assumptions). This was a major task, as many leading theorists were highly doubtful. It was also crucially important, for a model that is based on optimizing analysis is much more likely (according to the logic of mainstream economic analysis) to include private-sector equations that are invariant to policy behavior – i.e., that are not open to the "Lucas (1976) critique" – and therefore potentially satisfactory for analysis of alternative policies. But the book also does much more: For example, it shows how to extend the basic framework (1)-(3) in a tractable way that introduces "habit" behavior in spending, "inertia" in price adjustment, and "smoothing" in policy behavior. (Other extensions, such as endogenous investment, can also be accommodated.) Together, these steps make it possible for the resulting modification to match the dynamic properties of actual quarterly data reasonably well.[5]

In addition, the book shows how to obtain a central bank loss function consistent with policy designed to maximize utility of a typical household, while also yielding a policy rule of the same form as (3), often with extensions. The former step made it possible to view models of the NK type as empirically realistic, while the latter provided logical coherence to the entire approach, to an extent never before accomplished in monetary economics. The steps required some approximations along the way, but these were all analyzed in detail.[6]

### Misconceptions and Issues

Economists of all doctrinal varieties should and do admire Woodford's leading role in developing a framework that is: Based on optimizing analysis; reasonably consistent with data; realistic in its instrument specification; adaptable to extensions; and has an individual-utility basis for its policy rule. There is some unhappiness among a minority, nevertheless, over the small or non-existent role of money in the analysis. In part this stems from Michael's practice of beginning each major section of his book with analysis that represents a "cashless

economy," i.e., one in which there is no medium of exchange so the model's money serves only as a medium of account. To a considerable extent, this criticism is inappropriate. For in each chapter, Woodford goes back (after these beginnings) and repeats the analysis under the assumption that there are "transaction frictions" that money can help to overcome, thereby serving as a medium of exchange. In all these cases, he shows that, under plausible calibrations, the quantitative impact of including the medium-of-exchange function is very small. Nevertheless, it might have been a better procedure to begin with the case in which there are frictions, but ones that are virtually irrelevant for monetary policy because the function describing the frictions is additively separable. This would result in a model that would give rise to essentially the same conclusions, but would seem to partially defuse objections from the start.

In addition, I believe there is a degree of illogic in the "cashless" setup with money serving only as a medium of account. There are good reasons, both theoretical and empirical, for believing that when there is a medium of exchange, it will also serve as the economy's medium of account. But when there is no medium of exchange, there is little reason for confidence that the central bank-issued security, whose value the central bank manages, is one whose rate of interest is effective in governing aggregate demand.

One of the features of the New-Keynesian literature that I, like most academics, applaud, is its reliance on the assumption of rational expectations (RE), which is essentially the assumption that in forming expectations – as in other activities – purposeful individuals and firms behave so as to avoid *systematic* mistakes, even though random mistakes are inevitable. The whole science of economics rests on that

---

[5] At the price, of course, of some loss of analytical clarity and forcefulness.

[6] Woodford (2003) goes on to analyze – indeed, emphasize – "optimal" policy rules, to develop the "timeless perspective" approach to committed policy optimality, and to discuss many additional points of analytical and practical importance.

approximation. Also, it seems evident that no sensible policymaker would want to base his policy design on the assumption of any specific type of systematic mistake; for then the derived policy would try to exploit this pattern of mistakes and the agents would soon learn to behave differently. Some critics of RE contend, however, that it is unreasonable to conduct analysis "assuming that real-world agents believe that the economy functions in the way that the researcher's own particular model specifies." But that is *not* the logic of RE. It is, instead, that agents *in reality* succeed, by some process known only to themselves, in eliminating systematic components from their own expectational errors. The researcher proceeds with that assumption and must use *some* model; so he uses one that reflects his attempt to represent reality. Then it is logically implied that agents make mistakes only randomly with respect to this model – exactly the same assumption that applies to all other decisions made by households and firms.

Before closing, I would like to mention a few additional misconceptions regarding models of the type at hand. One line of criticism often heard in the United States, especially in the pages of *The Wall Street Journal*, concerns the role of price adjustment equation (2), which is then referred to as a "Phillips Curve," thereby evoking the discredited idea of a usable long-run trade-off. *The Wall Street Journal* position seems to be that the model should include *no* relationship of this sort. To me, that seems completely untenable, for what the Phillips Curve *is*, is a specification of the way in which the average price level adjusts when it differs from its *flexible-price* value. But such specification is needed, even if it is only that differences of this type never occur. The latter is a *coherent* position, but one that seems highly implausible – for it suggests that central banks cannot create recessions. Do its proponents believe that? I would think not, especially after the experience in the United States of the period 1980 to '83.

It might be added, that professional economists, including some excellent academics, have contributed to the terminological confusion regarding Phillips Curves by discussing their performance, be it good or bad, as a "model for forecasting inflation." But in a sensibly specified Phillips Curve relationship, there are two endogenous variables: The current inflation rate and also the current measure of the output gap. Thus, the Phillips Curve is not itself a complete model of inflation; it is only one of the relationships in a coherent model. It can be used as the sole relation involved in forecasting only by treating as exogenous (or predetermined) some variable(s) that should be treated as current endogenous.

There is, of course, scope for scholarly debate over the precise specification of the price adjustment relation. In the New-Keynesian literature some version of the Calvo (1983) model as in (2), is ubiquitous, in part because of the array of extensions and uses developed by Woodford in his book and elsewhere. (Many other economists have, of course, contributed important theoretical and empirical studies.) I have some reservations regarding it, but admire the work that has been done.

Another misconception occasionally found in *The Wall Street Journal* is that central banks should not try to conduct policy by way of interest rate manipulation because interest rates are fundamentally determined by financial markets, not the central bank. This objection, however, fails to distinguish between nominal and real interest rates. Clearly, monetary policy has ultimate power over the former; if the central bank creates a high inflation rate then the nominal interest rate will be high, with the real rate – determined largely by financial markets – not greatly changed. *If* the economy had perfect price flexibility, then the central bank would not be able to manage real rates, which are relevant for output determination. But even in this case it would be able to manage inflation!

There are also arguments over the third relation in the model, the intertemporal Euler equation (1), which has some empirical weaknesses. These mostly involve details about how to add richness and empirical verisimilitude to the specification, however, rather than fundamental disputes.

## Conclusion

Recent mainstream monetary policy analysis, which is well-represented by New-Keynesian models such as (1)-(3), combines theoretical rigor, concern for empirical veracity, and respect for actual central bank practice to an extent that represents an enormous improvement over the situation of 25 years ago, when Michael was a PhD student. There have been many important contributors to this development, but Michael Woodford has arguably been the most influential, and his *Interest and Prices* has almost certainly been the most outstanding publication in monetary economics over that time span.

**REFERENCES**

**Calvo, G. A.** 1983. "Staggered Prices in a Utility Maximizing Framework." *Journal of Monetary Economics*, 12(3): 383-398.

**Clarida, R., J. Galí, and M. Gertler.** 1999. "The Science of Monetary Policy: A New Keynesian Perspective." *Journal of Economic Literature*, 37(4): 1661–1707.

**Evans, G. W., and S. Honkapohja.** 2001. *Learning and Expectations in Macroeconomics.* Princeton, NJ: Princeton University Press.

**Goodfriend, M. and R. King.** 1997. "The New Neoclassical Synthesis and the Role of Monetary Policy." In *NBER macroeconomics annual 1997*, ed. B. S. Bernanke and J. J. Rotemberg, 231-83. Cambridge, MA: MIT Press.

**Lucas, R. E.** 1976. "Econometric Policy Evaluation: A Critique." *Carnegie-Rochester Conference Series on Public Policy*, 1(1): 19-46.

**McCallum, B. T.** 1985. "The Optimal Inflation Rate in an Overlapping-Generations Economy with Land." In *New Approaches to Monetary Economics*, ed. W.A. Barnett and K.J. Singleton, 325-339. New York: Cambridge University Press.

**McCallum, B. T.** 2003. "Is the Fiscal Theory of the Price Level Learnable?" *Scottish Journal of Political Economy*, 50: 634-49.

**Patinkin, D.** 1956. *Money, Interest, and Prices.* New York: Harper and Row.

**Taylor, J. B.** 1993. "Discretion Versus Policy Rules in Practice." *Carnegie-Rochester Conference Series on Public Policy*, 39(1): 195-214.

**Woodford, M.** 1985. "Credit Policy and the Price Level in a Cash-in-Advance Economy." In *New Approaches to Monetary Economics*, ed. W.A. Barnett and K.J. Singleton, 52-68. New York: Cambridge University Press.

**Woodford, M.** 1990. "Learning to Believe in Sunspots." *Econometrica*, 58(2): 277-307.

**Woodford, M.** 1995. "Price-Level Determinacy without Control of a Monetary Aggregate." *Carnegie-Rochester Conference Series on Public Policy*, 43(1): 1-46.

**Woodford, M.** 2003. *Interest and Prices: Foundations of a Theory of Monetary Policy.* Princeton, NJ: Princeton University Press.

**Woodford, M.** 2007. "How Important is Money in the Conduct of Monetary Policy?" NBER Working Paper 13325.

# THE NEW-KEYNESIAN APPROACH TO MONETARY POLICY ANALYSIS: LESSONS AND NEW DIRECTIONS*

Jordi Galí (CREI and Universitat Pompeu Fabra)

## The New-Keynesian Framework: Key Elements

The New-Keynesian (NK) approach to monetary policy analysis has emerged in recent years as one of the most influential and prolific areas of research in macroeconomics.[1] It has provided us with a framework that combines the theoretical rigor of Real Business Cycle (RBC) theory with Keynesian ingredients like monopolistic competition and nominal rigidities. That framework has also become the basis for the new generation of models being developed at central banks, and increasingly used for simulation and forecasting purposes.[2] In the present chapter, I will try to summarize what I view as some of the key lessons that have emerged from that research program and to point to some of the challenges it faces, as well as possible ways of overcoming these challenges.

Among the key defining features of the NK approach to monetary policy analysis the following seem worth emphasizing:

- It adopts many of the tools originally associated with RBC theory, including the systematic use of *dynamic stochastic general equilibrium (DSGE) models* based on optimizing behavior by households and firms, rational expectations, market clearing, etc.

- Firms are modelled as *monopolistic competitors,* i.e., each firm faces a well-defined demand schedule for the good it produces, and sets the price of that good (as opposed to taking it as given) in order to maximize its discounted profits.

- Nominal rigidities are a key element of the model and a main source of monetary policy non-neutrality. They are generally introduced in the form of constraints on the frequency

* Paper presented at the Center for Financial Studies Symposium on "The Science and Practice of Monetary Policy Today," Frankfurt, October 4, 2007. Much of the research described in this paper is based on joint work with Olivier Blanchard, Rich Clarida, and Mark Gertler, who should get credit for all the valuable insights. I remain solely responsible for any misrepresentation of that work.

[1] See Galí and Gertler (2007) for a quick introduction to the NK framework. The textbooks by Woodford (2003b) and Galí (2008) provide a more comprehensive treatment and analysis of the NK model.

[2] See, e.g., Smets and Wouters (2003, 2007).

with which firms and/or workers can adjust their nominal prices and wages, respectively. An implication of such constraints is that price and wage-setting decisions become forward-looking, since agents recognize that the prices/wages they set will remain effective beyond the current period.

- Emphasis is given to the endogenous component of monetary policy (i.e., monetary policy rules) and the consequences of alternative specifications of that component, rather than to the effects of exogenous changes in a monetary policy instrument.

- The NK framework can be used in order to evaluate the desirability of alternative policy rules, as well as to determine the optimality of such a rule, using a welfare-based criterion, based on the maximization of the utility of the economy's representative consumer, and in a way largely immune to the Lucas critique.

In addition to the previous elements, which are inherent to the basic NK model, one should emphasize that an important characteristic of the NK framework more generally lies in its proven flexibility to accommodate a large number of extensions to the basic model, including those incorporating open economy features, imperfect information and learning, unemployment, credit frictions, etc.

But what are the main insights that have emerged from the NK research program and what are some of the challenges it faces? This is the subject to which the present chapter is devoted. The lessons and novel insights I will focus on below pertain to the following topics:

- The costs of inflation and the benefits of price stability.
- The role of expectations and the gains from commitment.
- Importance of *"natural"* levels of output and

interest rates as policy benchmarks.
- The benefits of a *credible* anti-inflationary policy.

Before turning to a discussion of the above themes, I find it convenient to write down the three equations that constitute the simplest possible version of the NK model, and which I will use in subsequent sections to illustrate the main points I want to convey.

The first equation, usually referred to as the New-Keynesian Phillips Curve (NKPC), can be derived from the aggregation of the price-setting decisions by firms, combined with an equation describing the relationship between marginal cost and the level of activity. It takes the form:

$$\pi_t = \beta \, E_t \{\pi_{t+1}\} + \kappa \, x_t + u_t, \tag{1}$$

where $\pi_t$ is inflation, $x_t$ is the output gap, and $u_t$ is a cost-push shock. The output gap, $x_t \equiv y_t - y_t^n$, is defined as the difference between (log) output $y_t$ and the (log) natural level of output, $y_t^n$, where the latter corresponds to the level of output that would prevail in equilibrium in the absence of nominal frictions.

The second key block of the model relates the output gap positively to its expected one-period ahead value, and negatively to the interest rate gap, where the latter is defined as the difference between the real interest rate $i_t - E_t \{\pi_{t+1}\}$ and the natural rate of interest $r_t^n$, with the latter defined as the equilibrium real interest rate in the absence of nominal rigidities. The resulting equation is given by:

$$x_t = -\frac{1}{\sigma}(i_t - E_t \{\pi_{t+1}\} - r_t^n) + E_t \{x_{t+1}\}. \tag{2}$$

Finally, the model can be closed by means of a block describing how monetary policy is conducted. The simplest possible such description is given by a version of the so-called "Taylor rule", which takes the form:

$$i_t = \rho + \varnothing_\pi \pi_t + \varnothing_y \hat{y}_t + v_t,$$

where $i_t$ is the short-term nominal rate, and $\hat{y}_t$ represents deviations of (log) output from steady state (or trend level).

## The Costs of Inflation and the Benefits of Price Stability

What are the reasons why central banks should pursue a policy aimed at price stability? The NK framework provides a rigorous justification for such policies. To understand the main argument, let us assume at this point that there are no cost-push shocks, i.e. $u_t = 0$ for all t and that the presence of nominal rigidities is the only source of potential inefficiency in the level of output. In this case, and as captured by the NKPC (1), inflation will become an indicator of an inefficient level of activity, emerging from a deviation of output from its natural level caused by the presence of nominal rigidities. Thus, even if the central bank were not to care about inflation in itself, it will find its stabilization desirable as an indirect way to close the output gap. Furthermore, this will be possible even if the natural level of output (and thus the output gap) is unobservable.

But in addition to its role as a signal of an inefficient level of activity, the NK framework points to a more direct cost of inflation: It generates an inefficient allocation of resources across firms/sectors. To understand this channel, note that if there is positive inflation some firms must be raising their prices each period. But since not all firms can adjust their prices (or find it privately too costly to do so), relative prices will vary in ways not justified by sectoral or firm-level shocks, leading to suboptimal quantities of different goods being produced and consumed.

Note that a literal interpretation of the previous argument would call for zero inflation

to be sought at all times, independently of the costs in terms of employment or economic activity. But in practice several factors may call for maintaining a positive average level of inflation. These include the risk of hitting a zero lower bound on the nominal interest rate if the average level of the latter (which is related to average inflation) were to be too low. Also, the presence of downward nominal wage rigidities which may prevent warranted reductions in real wages in the absence of positive inflation. Furthermore, and independently of the desired level for average inflation, the presence of cost-push shocks generates a short-run trade-off between stabilization of inflation and stabilization of the output gap. To the extent that variations in both variables are independent sources of welfare losses (and under standard assumptions regarding the latter), it will be optimal for the central bank to accommodate some of the inflationary pressures.

Both considerations, taken together, suggest as a desirable policy the attainment of a positive target for inflation, over a medium-term horizon. That prescription appears to be consistent with the strategy followed by many central banks around the world.

## The Role of Expectations and the Gains from Commitment

The forward-looking nature of price setting and consumption decisions implies that both inflation and the output gap depend not only on the current value of their driving variables, but also on their anticipated future values. In other words, both inflation and the output gap are forward-looking variables. As a result, anticipated policy actions will have an influence on current outcomes, and thus the central bank may benefit from being able to influence related expectations. To illustrate this point, it is convenient to rewrite equations (1) and (2) as follows:

$$\pi_t = \kappa \, x_t + \kappa \sum_{k=1}^{\infty} \beta^k \, E_t \{x_{t+k}\} + u_t, \qquad (3)$$

$$x_t = -\frac{1}{\sigma} \, i_t - \frac{1}{\sigma} \sum_{k=1}^{\infty} E_t \{i_{t+k}\}$$

$$+ \frac{1}{\sigma} \sum_{k=1}^{\infty} E_t \{\pi_{t+k}\} + \frac{1}{\sigma} \, r_t^n. \qquad (4)$$

Suppose that an inflationary cost-push shock (i.e., a positive realization of $u_t$) hits the economy. In the absence of a commitment technology, the central bank can lower the current output gap in order to mitigate the impact of the shock on inflation. On the other hand, if the central bank can credibly commit to future state contingent actions, it can achieve the same inflation outcome with a smaller output gap decline by promising lower future output gaps, and thus driving down the expectational term in equation (3). To the extent that welfare losses are convex in the output gap, such a smoothing of the necessary output adjustment would be a more desirable strategy. Note, however, that such a policy will be time inconsistent: Once the shock has vanished, the central bank will be tempted to renege on its promises and stimulate the economy, bringing the output gap back to zero.[3]

A similar argument applies to the central bank's attempts to attain a given level of the output gap through changes in the interest rate: As (4) makes clear, it can do so by adjusting the current rate by a large amount or, alternatively, by smoothing the change over several periods, as long as it succeeds in convincing consumers (and firms, in a model with investment) that it will effectively do so. To the extent that fluctuations in interest rates generate welfare losses that are convex in the size of these fluctuations

the second strategy would generally be more desirable.[4]

More generally, the analysis of monetary policy in the context of a model with forward-looking variables points to the importance of credible commitment as a way to improve the central bank's current trade-offs. Communication with the public about the central bank's intentions takes a central role in this context. The current practice of central banks like the Reserve Bank of New Zealand, the Norges Bank, and the Riksbank of publishing the future interest rate path that is anticipated by the banks' decision makers themselves, given their current information, can be seen as an excellent illustration of expectations management at work.

## The Importance of Natural Levels as Policy Benchmarks

The natural levels of output and the interest rate play an important role in the design of monetary policy in the NK framework. Unfortunately, the inherent unobservability of these variables complicates their use in practice. Furthermore, their replacement by variables that may be viewed as proxies may do more harm than good.

A clear illustration of this problem can be found in the use of measures for the output gap. In numerous applications this variable is approximated by detrending (log) GDP using some statistical procedure, which generally associates the trend with a smooth function of time. By contrast, the benchmark used in the NK framework in order to determine the output gap is the natural level of output, which may display significant short-run fluctuations in response to all kinds of real shocks and, hence,

---

[3] See, e.g., Clarida, Galí and Gertler (1999) for an analysis of the optimal policy under commitment in the presence of cost-push shocks.
[4] See, e.g., Woodford (2003a).

is likely to be poorly approximated by a smooth function of time.[5]

In order to illustrate some of the potential consequences of using detrended output as a proxy for the output gap in implementation of policy, consider the problem of a central bank that seeks to minimize the loss function:

$$\sum_{t=0}^{\infty} (\alpha \, x_t^2 + \pi_t^2),$$

subject to (1). Let me restrict the analysis, for the sake of simplicity, to the case of no commitment, thus implying that the central bank takes expectations as given, effectively solving a sequence of static problems.[6] I also assume that $\{u_t\}$ and $\{y_t^n\}$ follow independent exogenous white noise processes.[7]

The optimality condition for this problem is given by:

$$x_t = -\frac{\kappa}{\alpha} \pi_t, \qquad (5)$$

for all t. Substituting this optimality condition into (1) and solving for inflation we obtain:

$$\pi_t = \frac{\alpha}{\alpha + \kappa^2} u_t,$$

which combined with (5) yields:

$$x_t = -\frac{\kappa}{\alpha + \kappa^2} u_t.$$

The implied standard deviations of inflation and the output gap are thus given by:

$$\sigma (\pi_t) = \frac{\alpha}{\alpha + \kappa^2} \sigma (u_t),$$

$$\sigma (x_t) = \frac{\kappa}{\alpha + \kappa^2} \sigma (u_t).$$

Suppose next that, given the unobservability of the output gap, the central bank replaces it with detrended GDP when trying to implement

optimality condition (5). Thus we have:

$$\hat{y}_t = -\frac{\kappa}{\alpha} \pi_t,$$

or, equivalently,

$$x_t = -\frac{\kappa}{\alpha} \pi_t - \hat{y}_t^n. \qquad (6)$$

Combining (6) with (1) we can solve for the implied equilibrium levels of inflation and the output gap under the "approximate" optimal rule, which yields:

$$\pi_t = \frac{\alpha}{\alpha + \kappa^2} (u_t - \kappa \, \hat{y}_t^n),$$

and

$$x_t = -\frac{1}{\alpha + \kappa^2} (\kappa \, u_t + \alpha \, \hat{y}_t^n).$$

Thus, the implied volatility for the output gap and inflation are now given by:

$$\sigma (\pi_t) = \frac{\alpha}{\alpha + \kappa^2} \sigma (u_t) + \frac{\alpha\kappa}{\alpha + \kappa^2} \sigma(\hat{y}_t^n),$$

$$\sigma (x_t) = \frac{\kappa}{\alpha + \kappa^2} \sigma (u_t) + \frac{\alpha}{\alpha + \kappa^2} \sigma(\hat{y}_t^n).$$

Thus, we see that the focus on detrended output instead of the output gap leads to higher volatility in both inflation and the output gap, and hence, to greater welfare losses. Note that the additional welfare losses are proportional to $\sigma(\hat{y}_t^n)$, which measures the variability of the natural level of output. The intuition for this result comes from the fact that, under (5), the central bank fully accommodates all the variations in the natural level of output, keeping inflation and the output gap unchanged. By contrast, the adoption of (6) as a rule has the consequence (albeit unintentional) of smoothing output variations excessively, even when the latter are backed by changes in the

---

[5] See Galí and Gertler (1998) for a discussion of the implications of using detrended GDP in empirical evaluations of the New-Keynesian Phillips Curve.
[6] See Clarida, Galí, and Gertler (1999) for a more detailed analysis of that problem.
[7] The generalization to AR(1) processes is straightforward and yields no additional insights.

natural level of output. Note, finally, that the excess volatility created by the implementation of the "approximate" rule is increasing in the weight attached to output gap variability in the loss function.

The previous example illustrates the potential usefulness of measures of the natural level of output in the implementation of monetary policy. A similar case can be made for the natural interest rate: One can show that, under the model assumptions made above, the optimal discretionary policy can be implemented by means of an interest rate rule of the form:

$$i_t = r_t^n + \varnothing_\pi \pi_t,$$

with $\varnothing_\pi \equiv \dfrac{\sigma \kappa}{\alpha}$.[8] Note that the previous rule requires that the central bank adjusts the nominal rate one-for-one in response to variations in the natural rate. That policy is hampered in practice by the unobservability of the latter.

The importance of natural levels of output and the interest rate makes the development of estimated DSGE models particularly useful, since such models can be used to make inferences (however imprecise) regarding these variables. Perhaps not surprisingly, the behavior of the output gap measures that have been backed out from some of the existing estimated DSGE models has little resemblance to the ones obtained using traditional detrending approaches or an earlier generation of models.[9]

---

### The Benefits of a Credible Anti-Inflationary Policy

---

Next I illustrate the benefits of credibility when pursuing a strong anti-inflationary

policy. Suppose that the economy is, once again, described by equations (1) and (2).[10] The central bank follows a simple interest rate rule of the form:

$$i_t = \rho + \varnothing_\pi \pi_t, \tag{7}$$

where $\varnothing_\pi > 1$. The public, however, believes the rule is given by:

$$i_t = \rho + \varnothing_\pi (1 - \delta) \pi_t + v_t, \tag{8}$$

where $\delta$ is a constant that can be interpreted as a "credibility gap," measuring the extent to which the public "discounts" the central bank's anti-inflation stance. The error term $v_t$ is taken to be an exogenous policy shock, following a white noise process. Finally, it is assumed that

$$\varnothing_\pi (1 - \delta) > 1.$$

I solve for the equilibrium of the model by combining (1), (2), and (8), for an arbitrary white noise process $\{v_t\}$, and under the assumption that the cost-push shock $\{u_t\}$ follows an AR(1) process with autoregressive coefficient $\rho_u$. For simplicity, I assume a constant natural interest rate $r_t^n = \rho$. The resulting equilibrium, which can be easily solved for using the method of undetermined coefficients, is given by:

$$\pi_t = a\, u_t + b\, v_t,$$

$$x_t = c\, u_t + d\, v_t,$$

where $a \equiv \dfrac{\sigma(1 - \rho_u)}{\sigma(1 - \rho_u)(1 - \beta \rho_u) + \kappa[\varnothing_\pi(1 - \delta) - \rho_u]}$,

$$b \equiv -\dfrac{\kappa}{\sigma + \kappa \varnothing_\pi(1 - \delta)},$$

$$c \equiv -\dfrac{\varnothing_\pi(1 - \delta) - \rho_u}{\sigma(1 - \rho_u)(1 - \beta \rho_u) + \kappa[\varnothing_\pi(1 - \delta) - \rho_u]},$$

and $d \equiv -\dfrac{1}{\sigma + \kappa \varnothing_\pi(1 - \delta)}.$

---

[8] The desired allocation will be the unique equilibrium if $\alpha < \sigma \kappa$, i.e. if the interest rate rule satisfies the so-called "Taylor principle".
[9] See, e.g., Edge, Kiley and Laforte (2007).
[10] The exercise presented here is based on Blanchard and Galí (2007b).

Given that the central bank truly follows (7) it must be the case that, ex-post, $v_t = \delta \varnothing_\pi \pi_t$ for all t. We can then impose this on the equilibrium conditions above to obtain final expressions for inflation and the output gap as functions of the cost-push shock:

$$\pi_t = \frac{a}{1 - \delta \varnothing_\pi b}\, u_t,$$

$$x_t = \left(c + \frac{\delta \varnothing_\pi da}{1 - \delta \varnothing_\pi b}\right) u_t.$$

In oder to determine the impact of the credibility gap on the trade-off facing the central bank, I compute the standard deviations of inflation and the output gap, $\sigma(\pi_t)$ and $\sigma(x_t)$, implied by the previous expressions for a calibrated version of the model. In particular, I assume $\beta = 0.99$, $\kappa = 0.1$, $\sigma = 1$, $\sigma(u_t) = 0.25$ and $\rho_u = 0.9$; all of which are kept unchanged. I then consider two values for the credibility gap: $\delta = 0.5$ and $\delta = 0$, with the latter corresponding to the full credibility benchmark. *Figure 1* shows, for each value of $\delta$ considered, the locus of feasible combinations of $\sigma(\pi_t)$ and $\sigma(x_t)$ given the interest rate rule (7), with that locus being spanned by varying $\varnothing_\pi$ over its admissible range.[11]

*Figure 1*

**Policy Credibility and Macroeconomic Volatility**

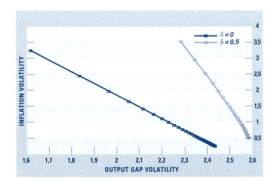

As *Figure 1* makes clear, an improvement in credibility (captured here by a decline in $\delta$ from 0.5 to 0) makes it possible, through an appropriate choice of $\varnothing_\pi$, to reduce simultaneously the volatility of both inflation and the output gap. In other words, there are potential welfare gains to be made if the central bank conveys in a *credible* way the degree of its anti-inflationary stance. By appearing more dovish than the central bank actually is, the trade-off it faces between stabilization of inflation and stabilization of the output gap is likely to worsen.

---

### Sources of Policy Trade-offs in the New-Keynesian Framework: A Challenge?

Despite the overall success of the NK research program and the favorable assessment of the ability of medium-scale versions of the NK model, several challenges remain. Here, I briefly discuss one such challenge which was the focus of Blanchard and Galí (2007a): The need to uncover relevant sources of policy trade-offs.

While the analysis above has made use of a version of the New-Keynesian Phillips Curve (given by (1)) that incorporates a trade-off between output gap and inflation stabilization in the form of an exogenous cost-push shock $u_t$, what the latter represents is often far from clear. In fact, the inflation equation that emerges in the baseline NK model lacks that feature and takes instead the form:

$$\pi_t = \beta \, E_t \{\pi_{t+1}\} + \kappa \, (y_t - y_t^n). \qquad (9)$$

Note that, under (9), inflation occurs if and only if the level of output is above its corresponding level with flexible prices. The reason is that only in this case (and under standard assumptions) will average markups

---

[11] The standard deviation of inflation is multiplied by 4 so that it corresponds to a measure of inflation expressed in annual rates.

be lower than desired and, as a result, firms that adjust their prices will tend to increase the latter, generating inflation.

Furthermore, in standard versions of the NK framework, the underlying real model implies a constant gap between the natural (i.e., flexible price) output $y_t^n$ and the efficient output, $y_t^e$. This gap is a consequence of the presence of monopolistic competition (with constant desired markups) in goods markets which, if uncorrected, makes output inefficiently low even in the absence of nominal rigidities. Formally,

$$y_t^e - y_t^n = \delta.$$

Combining both equations, we obtain:

$$\pi_t = \beta \ E_t \{\pi_{t+1}\} + \kappa \ (y_t - y_t^e + \delta), \quad (10)$$

which makes clear the absence of a trade-off between stabilization of inflation and stabilization of the welfare-relevant output gap, where the latter is defined as the (log) deviation between output and the efficient level of output.

The lack of such a trade-off, a property which Blanchard and Galí (2007a) refer to as "the divine coincidence," implies that central banks should focus on completely stabilizing inflation, period by period, and with no concern for the output or employment losses that such a policy might bring about. The reason is that, according to the above framework, the resulting fluctuations in these variables would reflect, one-for-one, movements in their efficient levels. That implication is clearly at odds with conventional wisdom as well as with the practice of most central banks, including those that claim to follow an inflation targeting strategy. In practice, attainability of the inflation objective is understood to refer to the medium

run, but not necessarily "continuously," as the model without a trade-off would imply.

A number of solutions to the above problem have been proposed in the literature. The simplest one, adopted in earlier sections of the present chapter, consists in appending an exogenous disturbance to inflation equation (10). That disturbance can be interpreted as resulting from exogenous variations in distortionary taxes, and/or exogenous changes in desired wage and price markups.[12] Such factors would lead to exogenous variations in the gap between the efficient and natural levels of output and, hence, to an inflation equation of the form:

$$\pi_t = \beta \ E_t \{\pi_{t+1}\} + \kappa \ (y_t - y_t^e) + \kappa \ \delta_t,$$

with the consequent policy trade-offs. Yet, that solution seems unsatisfactory, since it restricts the existence of meaningful policy trade-offs to shocks that are unlikely to be major drivers of macro fluctuations.

The introduction of staggered nominal wage setting, as in Erceg, Henderson, and Levin (2000), while leaving unaltered the property of a constant gap between $y_t^e$ and $y_t^n$, generates a trade-off between price inflation and the welfare relevant output gap, as a consequence of the *endogenous* variations in wage markups resulting from the sluggish adjustment of nominal wages. Yet, this trade-off is somewhat apparent since it is possible to derive an equation for a particular weighted average of price and wage inflation, $\bar{\pi}_t$, which takes the same form as (10), with $\bar{\pi}_t$ replacing $\pi_t$. Most importantly, and as discussed in Erceg et al. (2000) and Woodford (2003b), complete stabilization of the welfare relevant output gap (and, hence, of the specific weighted average of price and wage inflation) is nearly optimal in this model. Thus, once again, the central bank should focus exclusively on

---

[12] See, e.g., Steinsson (2003).

fully stabilizing an inflation measure, period by period, without concern for the output and employment consequences of such a policy. In that sense, the model lacks a meaningful policy trade-off.

---

### An Alternative Approach:
### Real Imperfections as a Source
### of Policy Trade-offs

---

In a recent paper with Olivier Blanchard, we have proposed an alternative source of monetary policy trade-offs, resulting from the existence of *real imperfections*. The latter may lead to inefficient responses to shocks, *even in the absence of nominal rigidities*.[13] In other words, and using the terminology introduced above, the natural level of output and the efficient level of output may not adjust by the same amount in response to different real shocks. As a result, the gap $y_t^e - y_t^n$ will vary endogenously, with the implied inflation equation being:

$$\pi_t = \beta \, E_t \{\pi_{t+1}\} + \kappa \, (y_t - y_t^e) + u_t,$$

with

$$u_t \equiv \kappa \, (y_t^e - y_t^n).$$

In this context, it is clear that an endogenous trade-off between inflation and output gap stabilization will emerge, with *strict* inflation targeting being no longer optimal.

What are examples of real imperfections that are likely to generate such trade-offs? In a series of recent papers with Olivier Blanchard we have focused on slow adjustment of real wages as such an imperfection.[14] In particular, if the real wage responds less than one-for-one to changes in the marginal rate of substitution when a supply shock (e.g., an increase in the price of oil) hits the economy, the natural level of output will display excessive fluctuations

relative to the efficient level of output. Fully stabilizing inflation would require closing the gap between output and its natural level, which would thus generate welfare-reducing fluctuations in the gap between output and its efficient counterpart. A strict inflation targeting policy will generally not be optimal in this context. Instead, the optimal policy will generally involve a partial accommodation of inflationary pressures in the short-run, with inflation returning to its long-term target level only gradually.

One can imagine other real imperfections that would have analogous implications. Consider, for instance, a model with credit market imperfections along the lines of Bernanke, Gertler and Gilchrist (1999), in which there is an external finance premium (i.e., the wedge between the interest rate charged to firms to finance their investment projects and the consumer's marginal rate of intertemporal substitution) which is decreasing in net worth. The resulting model generates a financial accelerator mechanism: In the absence of nominal rigidities, adverse shocks will lead to a reduction in net worth and, consequently, an increase in the external finance premium and an inefficiently large reduction in investment and output. In the presence of nominal rigidities, there is room for monetary policy to affect the level of economic activity and thus to alleviate such excessive fluctuations. Doing so, however, would require deviating from a strict inflation targeting policy, since the latter will generally bring about the flexible price equilibrium allocation. Early explorations of the consequences of credit market frictions for the design of monetary policy can be found in Christiano, Motto, and Rostagno (2006), Faia and Monacelli (2006), Gilchrist and Leahy (2002), and Monacelli (2006).

---

[13] See Blanchard and Galí (2007).
[14] See Blanchard and Galí (2006, 2007a, 2007b).

## Concluding Remarks

In the present chapter I have discussed some of the lessons for monetary policy that have emerged from the New-Keynesian research program. These lessons include, but are not restricted to, the benefits of price stability, the gains from commitment about future policies, the importance of natural variables as benchmarks for policy, and the benefits of a credible anti-inflationary stance. I have also pointed to one challenge facing NK modelling efforts – the need to come up with relevant sources of meaningful policy trade-offs – and briefly discussed a potentially fruitful approach to meeting that challenge, based on the introduction of real imperfections which create an endogenous time-varying wedge between the efficient and natural levels of output.

In spite of some of the challenges and shortcomings of the NK approach, I believe the overall verdict is a positive one. It has generated many novel insights that appear to be relevant for the design and practical conduct of monetary policy. It also provides a coherent framework to organize our thinking about the workings of the economy and to provide internally consistent accounts of actual macroeconomic developments. Furthermore, the NK framework has proved to be a very flexible tool, capable of accommodating a large number of features missing from the basic model, including open economy factors, imperfect information and learning, unemployment, credit frictions, etc. Finally, the ongoing adoption of the NK framework as the core of the medium-scale models under development at central banks and other institutions guarantees that at least some of the quantitative analysis undertaken at these institutions, whether aimed at policy simulation or forecasts, is backed by rigorous theoretical macro modelling. Time will tell whether central banks end up finding that quantitative analysis useful, but I think there are reasons to be optimistic as long as the expectations are not set too high. After all, even in its rich incarnation full of bells and whistles, the NK model is still a highly stylized representation of the economy, so one must be aware of its limitations. But it is certainly an improvement over purely statistical models or the old-fashioned, largely atheoretical macroeconometric models of the not so distant past.

# REFERENCES

**Bayoumi, T.** 2004. "GEM: A New International Macroeconomic Model." IMF Occasional Paper no. 239.

**Bernanke, B., M. Gertler, and S. Gilchrist.** 1999. "The Financial Accelerator in a Quantitative Business Cycle Framework." In *Handbook of Macroeconomics*, ed. J. Taylor and M. Woodford, volume 1C, 1341-1397. New York: Elsevier.

**Blanchard, O. J., and J. Galí.** 2006. "A New Keynesian Model with Unemployment." mimeo.

**Blanchard, O. J., and J. Galí.** 2007a. "Real Wage Rigidities and the New Keynesian Model." *Journal of Money, Credit, and Banking*, 39(s1): 35-66.

**Blanchard, O. J., and J. Galí.** 2007b. "The Macroeconomic Effects of Oil Shocks: Why are the 2000s so Different from the 1970s?" NBER Working Paper no. 13668.

**Christiano, L. J., R. Motto, and M. Rostagno.** 2006. "Monetary Policy and Stock Market Boom-Bust Cycles." mimeo.

**Clarida, R., J. Galí, and M. Gertler.** 1999. "The Science of Monetary Policy: A New Keynesian Perspective." *Journal of Economic Literature*, 37(4): 1661-1707.

**Edge, R. M., M. T. Kiley, and J.-P. Laforte.** 2007. "Documentation of the Research and Statistics Division's Estimated DSGE Model of the U.S. Economy: 2006 Version." Finance and Economics Discussion Series 2007-53, Federal Reserve Board, Washington D.C.

**Erceg, C. J., D. W. Henderson, and A. T. Levin.** 2000. "Optimal Monetary Policy with Staggered Wage and Price Contracts." *Journal of Monetary Economics*, 46(2): 281-314.

**Faia, E., and T. Monacelli.** 2006. "Optimal Interest Rate Rules, Asset Prices and Credit Frictions." *Journal of Economic Dynamics and Control*, 31(10): 3228-3254.

**Galí, J.** 2008. Forthcoming. *Monetary Policy, Inflation, and the Business Cycle. An Introduction to the New Keynesian Framework and its Monetary Policy Applications.* Princeton, NJ: Princeton University Press.

**Galí, J., and M. Gertler.** 1999. "Inflation Dynamics: A Structural Econometric Analysis." *Journal of Monetary Economics*, 44(2): 195-222.

**Galí, J., and M. Gertler.** 2007. "Macroeconomic Modeling for Monetary Policy Evaluation." *Journal of Economic Perspectives*, 21(4): 25-45.

**Gilchrist, S., and J. Leahy.** 2002. "Monetary Policy and Asset Prices." *Journal of Monetary Economics*, 49 (1): 75-97.

**Monacelli, T.** 2006. "Optimal Monetary Policy with Collateralized Household Debt and Borrowing Constraints." mimeo.

**Nakamura, E., and J. Steinsson.** 2006. "Five Facts about Prices: A Reevaluation of Menu Costs Models." Harvard University, mimeo.

**Smets, F., and R. Wouters.** 2003. "An Estimated Dynamic Stochastic General Equilibrium Model of the Euro Area." *Journal of the European Economic Association*, 1(5): 1123-1175.

**Smets, F., and R. Wouters.** 2007. "Shocks and Frictions in US Business Cycles: a Bayesian DSGE Approach." *American Economic Review*, 97(3): 586-606.

**Steinsson, J.** 2003. "Optimal Monetary Policy in an Economy with Inflation Persistence." *Journal of Monetary Economics*, 50(7): 1425-1456.

**Woodford, M.** 2001. "The Taylor Rule and Optimal Monetary Policy." *American Economic Review*, 91(2): 232-237.

**Woodford, M.** 2003a. "Optimal Interest Rate Smoothing." *Review of Economic Studies*, 70(4): 861-886.

**Woodford, M.** 2003b. *Interest and Prices: Foundations of a Theory of Monetary Policy.* Princeton, NJ: Princeton University Press.

# THE NEW-KEYNESIAN APPROACH IN FORECASTING AND MONETARY POLICY DESIGN

# THE CASE FOR FORECAST TARGETING AS A MONETARY POLICY STRATEGY*

Michael Woodford (Columbia University)

At central banks around the world, forecasts have come to play an increasingly important role both in policy deliberations and in communications with the public. The most striking examples are the Bank of England, Sweden's Riksbank, Norway's Norges Bank, and the Reserve Bank of New Zealand, all of which conduct policy on the basis of a procedure sometimes referred to as "inflation-forecast targeting" (Svensson, 1997, 1999). Under this approach, the central bank constructs quantitative projections of the economy's expected future evolution based on the way in which it intends to control short-term interest rates, and public discussion of those projections is a critical part of the way in which the bank justifies the conduct of policy to the public.

What accounts for the appeal of a forecast-targeting approach, and should it be adopted more widely or more explicitly? I begin by reviewing the long-running debate between the proponents of monetary rules, intended to ensure confidence in the value of money over time, and the proponents of discretionary monetary policy, aimed at stabilizing the real economy. I will argue that inflation-forecast targeting represents a powerful synthesis of the two approaches; in particular, it is an improvement both over simpler rules, such as targeting a monetary aggregate, and over weaker versions of inflation targeting. I shall also argue that a much more extensive communication policy is crucial to escaping from the limitations of the traditional alternatives of rigid rules or rudderless discretion.

I will then explore some common questions that arise about inflation-forecast targeting. Should only the inflation forecast matter, and if not, in what way should forecasts of other economic variables affect policy decisions? What assumptions about the course of future policy should be used in constructing the quantitative projections that are presented to the public? Finally, given that economic forecasts always have an element of inaccuracy – and may even be subject to persistent bias for a time – is a forecast-based approach really as reliable as adherence to a simpler rule, if one's primary concern is the avoidance of major errors like the Great Inflation of the 1970s? I conclude with some thoughts about how the U.S. Federal Reserve might move toward an explicit policy of inflation-forecast targeting.

* Paper first published in *Journal of Economic Perspectives*, Volume 21, Number 4, Fall 2007, pp. 3-24.

## Beyond the Antinomy
## of Rules versus Discretion

I shall argue that inflation-forecast targeting represents a synthesis of two apparently antithetical conceptions of good monetary policy. The first ideal is the quest for a *monetary standard*, an arrangement that serves to guarantee a stable value for a particular monetary unit over the foreseeable future. The primary aim of a monetary standard is to install confidence regarding the future value of money. Because of the importance attached to instilling and maintaining confidence, rigid rules are often argued to be necessary so that the monetary authority's conformity with the rules can constantly be made manifest. The second ideal is that of *monetary stabilization policy*, according to which judicious adjustment of monetary policy in response to varying economic conditions can help to stabilize the real economy or, more precisely, to ensure an optimal adjustment to economic disturbances despite lags in the adjustment of nominal wages and prices. Effective monetary stabilization policy requires flexibility in the way that policy may respond to differing circumstances, and as a consequence, the proponents of stabilization policy frequently argue for the importance of allowing central bankers considerable discretion in the decisions that they make at any given time.

These two ideals are often presented as irreconcilable. The choice is often described as being between "rules" and "discretion," with each term being defined by its denial of the other. Yet a deeper analysis of the two ideals reveals less incompatibility between them. In fact, one of the principal benefits of a monetary standard – which is to say, of a regime that provides a clear anchor for expectations regarding the future value of money – is a

greater scope for the use of monetary policy for short-run stabilization of the real economy.

Research in monetary economics over the past few decades – including the work for which Milton Friedman, Edmund Phelps, and Robert Lucas have now all been awarded Nobel Prizes – has shown that the short-run trade-off between inflation and real activity, which provides the basis for the effects of monetary policy on real activity, depends critically on *inflation expectations*. An increased expected rate of inflation results in a higher rate of current inflation being required for a given level of real activity. It follows that if expectations are not firmly anchored, and thus are easily shifted in response to variations in the observed rate of inflation, then short-run variations in the rate of inflation will *not* produce substantial differences between current inflation and expected inflation, and hence will have only a small effect on real activity. However, if people have reason to believe that inflation will always return fairly quickly to a stable long-run rate, so that an observed departure of the current inflation rate from the average rate has little effect on expected inflation for the future, the short-run "Phillips-curve" trade-off between inflation and employment is much flatter, allowing monetary policy a larger short-run effect on real activity.[1] Hence even from the point of view of improved stabilization of the real economy, it is important to find a way of stabilizing inflation expectations.

Some might conclude from this that one goal for monetary policy should have an absolute priority over the other: That one should choose a monetary regime solely with a view to its consequences for long-run price stability, and allow the central bank to disclaim any responsibility for fluctuations in business activity. But there is no necessary conflict

---

[1] Bank of England Governor Mervyn King (2005) argues that tighter anchoring of the public's inflation expectations has made possible greater stability of *both* real activity and inflation since the introduction of inflation targeting in the United Kingdom. *Figure 7* of Benati (2006) offers evidence of shifts in the slope of the U.K. Phillips curve across alternative monetary regimes consistent with the mechanism sketched in the text.

between a sensible degree of concern for stabilization of the real economy — one that is consistent with a sound understanding of what monetary policy can actually accomplish — and the pursuit of a policy that ensures stability of the value of money over the medium to long-run. Suppositions to the contrary are based on too narrow a view of the possible bases for confidence in the future purchasing power of money.

A traditional view has been that confidence in a monetary standard should derive from a commitment to convertibility of the currency into something else of known value. Typically, this was a precious metal, gold having been the most popular choice, though there were also experiments with silver standards, bimetallic standards, and so on. The classical gold standard did succeed in keeping the cumulative increase in the general price level in the United States near zero from 1776 to 1914. But the relative price-inelasticity of both the supply of gold and of the nonmonetary demand for gold means that the relative price of gold can vary widely for many years at a time, so that stabilizing the dollar price of gold implies little stability for the prices of other goods and services, except over the very long-run. Thus, this approach to the maintenance of confidence in the long-run value of the monetary unit has a serious cost: Policy is completely subordinated to the achievement of a criterion (a fixed dollar value of gold) that is not very closely related to one's true stabilization objectives, simply on the ground that conformity to this kind of commitment is easily verifiable.

After the final abandonment of any connection of the world's currencies to gold in the early 1970s, a widely advocated alternative approach to guaranteeing the value of money was money-growth targeting. Proponents argued that both the likelihood of achieving inflation control and the visibility of a central bank's commitment to controlling inflation would be increased by the adoption of an "intermediate target" for something that the central bank could more directly control than the rate of inflation itself, but that was nonetheless reliably connected to inflation, at least over long enough periods of time. Once again, however, choice of a target that allows relatively straightforward verification of compliance with the commitment conflicts with the choice of one that is closely related to reasonable stabilization objectives, other than at very low frequencies.

A narrow definition of money, like the monetary base, can be closely controlled by the central bank, making verification of compliance simple; but the link between this measure of money and aggregate expenditure can fluctuate considerably. Broader definitions of money, like the M3 measure emphasized by the European Central Bank, are somewhat more reliably connected to the volume of nominal expenditure, but the central bank has less direct influence upon these broader measures of the money supply. Moreover, regardless of the narrowness or breadth of monetary aggregate that one chooses to target, the connection between stable money growth and stability of either inflation or aggregate expenditure has turned out to be shaky, except over fairly long periods of time. Money-demand relations have proven to be particularly unstable in recent decades (Friedman and Kuttner, 1996; Estrella and Mishkin, 1997), as a consequence of rapid innovation in financial arrangements, and as a result, few central banks currently pay much attention to monetary aggregates in judging the appropriateness of their policy stance.[2]

But are mechanical rules of these kinds the only way of creating confidence that a central bank will maintain a predictable rate of inflation over the medium to long-run? The problem is

---

[2] The European Central Bank is an obvious exception, at least as far as public rhetoric is concerned. But even there, the bank's "reference value" for M3 growth has played at most a minor role in actual policy decisions (Fischer, Lenza, Pill, and Reichlin, 2006).

surely not a lack of any other effective *means* through which a central bank that wishes to do so can guarantee a desired long-run average inflation rate. This problem is not a difficult one: As long as a central bank possesses a reasonably reliable measure of the price level (with only a modest delay) and some instrument that can influence the rate of inflation (at least eventually) with a known sign, then it is surely possible to offset any past tendency to drift away from the target inflation so as to ensure that no deviation persists unchecked for many years. The only real challenge – at least where long-run price stability is concerned – is one of making *visible* to the public the central bank's commitment to act in this way.

A mechanical rule has a certain advantage in this regard, since it should be possible to observe fairly directly whether it is being followed. But there is an alternative way of addressing the problem, which is to commit to *explaining* publicly the basis for the central bank's decisions. A more sophisticated policy – one that aims to stabilize the real economy to some extent in the short-run, but in a way that is consistent with maintaining a relatively constant inflation rate over a period of several years – is possible in principle, and it should be possible to pursue such a policy without sacrificing the possibility of stable medium-run inflation expectations, as long as the central bank can show the public that its actions are consistent with a strategy of this kind and ensure that people understand what the consequences of such a strategy should be.

The key to avoiding the disadvantages of a mechanical rule, without allowing the drift in inflationary expectations that occurs all too easily under a purely discretionary policy, is thus a commitment to *explain* the policy decisions that are made. While a good policy may well take into account the effects of policy on the real economy, it must do so in a way that does not imply instability in the medium-

term inflation outlook. While a good policy may well respond to a wide range of sources of information about the economy's current state, it must do so in accordance with a consistent strategy that private decisionmakers can rely upon in forecasting future conditions. Above all, these aspects of the policy strategy must be made visible to the public. This is where forecast-based monetary policy has a crucial advantage: Not simply in helping to improve the accuracy of central bank judgments about how to best achieve the bank's stabilization objectives, but also in explaining the character of that policy to the public.

## Inflation-Forecast Targeting

Since the early 1990s, inflation-forecast targeting has rapidly gained popularity as an alternative to monetary policy strategies based either on monetary aggregates or convertibility. When referring to inflation-forecast targeting, I mean not just the public announcement of an inflation target – though that is certainly a crucial element – but also a commitment to a specific structured approach to deliberations about monetary policy actions and a corresponding framework for communication about the justification for those actions. A central bank that practices inflation-forecast targeting is committed to adjusting its instrument or instruments of policy (typically, this means its operating target for an overnight interest rate) in whatever way proves to be necessary in order to ensure that the bank's quantitative *projections* of the economy's future evolution satisfy a specific *target criterion*.

For example, the Bank of England has often stated that its monetary policy is intended to satisfy the requirement that the projection for a particular measure of inflation (currently, one based on a consumer price index) equal 2.0 percent at a horizon eight quarters in the future. Although this description is plainly an

*Figure 1*

**The "Fan Charts" from the *Inflation Report* of the Bank of England**

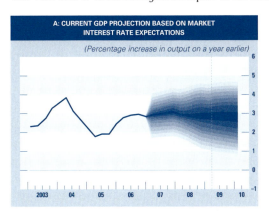

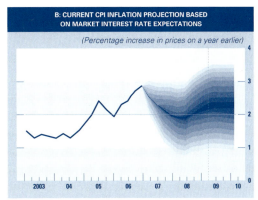

**Source:** *Figures 1A* and *1B* reproduce Charts 1 and 2 from the introduction of the May 2007 *Inflation Report* of the Bank of England.
**Notes:** The "fan chart" in *Figure 1A* indicates a probability distribution of possible future evolutions of GDP over a three-year horizon, while the fan chart in *Figure 1B* shows a probability distribution of possible future evolutions of inflation, with the modal projection indicated by the most deeply shaded region. The CPI is the Consumer Price Index.

oversimplification of the Bank's actions, each issue of the Bank's quarterly *Inflation Report* begins with an overview of the justification of the current stance of policy that contains two charts like those shown in *Figure 1*. The "fan chart" in *Figure 1A* indicates a probability distribution of possible future evolutions of GDP over a three-year horizon, while the fan chart in *Figure 1B* shows a probability distribution of possible future evolutions of inflation, with the modal projection indicated by the most deeply shaded region. Primary emphasis is given to *Figure 1B* in judging that the evolution of policy assumed in constructing the projections is suitable (more on that below!); the vertical dashed line at a horizon eight quarters in the future and the horizontal line at the inflation target of 2.0 percent help the eye to judge whether the path of deepest shading crosses the intersection.

This forward-looking decision procedure allows the central bank to use *all* available information about the current outlook for the economy, including non-quantitative information ("judgment"), in determining the appropriate level of interest rates. There is a specific target criterion, which favors both focus in the decision-making process and predictability of the policy committee's decisions, but the criterion involves the central bank's actual stabilization goals rather than an "intermediate target," like a monetary aggregate that is of little independent interest. Inflation-forecast targeting is not tied to a mechanical formula that makes monetary policy a function of some very small set of present economic variables (like a "Taylor rule" for monetary policy).[3] After all, the relation of current economic variables to the variable that one actually wishes to stabilize may change over time.

Inflation-forecast targeting also involves a commitment to regular publication of the projections on the basis of which policy decisions have been made, typically through reports (like the *Inflation Report* of the Bank of England) published several times per year. Such publications serve the goal of anchoring inflation expectations in several ways. First, they make the central bank's policy commitment verifiable, by allowing the public to see at frequent intervals

---

[3] In John Taylor's (1993) celebrated rule of thumb for Fed policy, the Federal Funds Rate should be a linear function of inflation over the previous four quarters and the current output gap.

that policy is still being conducted in a manner consistent with that commitment. In addition, they sharpen expectations about the likely future conduct of policy by allowing people to observe how the central bank processes and responds to developments of various types (the import of which for the bank's projections and decisions are discussed in the report). Finally, publication of the bank's own view of the future outlook for inflation can directly influence inflation expectations. In particular, a chart might show why a current inflation rate that is different from the target rate (and perhaps even moving in the wrong direction, as in the corresponding chart from the Bank of England's November 2006 report) is nonetheless consistent with an expectation that inflation will be close to the target rate within a few years, and this information can help to keep medium-run inflation expectations anchored, despite the highfrequency variations that tend to dominate press coverage. The justification of policy decisions by reference to quantitative projections is a crucial feature of this policy strategy, for these projections are expected to substitute for verification of convertibility (as under a gold standard) or verification of conformity with an "intermediate target" (such as a money-growth target) as a basis for the public's confidence in the future value of money.

Can inflation-forecast targeting really succeed in anchoring inflation expectations in the way that one demands of a monetary standard, while simultaneously allowing the flexibility required for a reasonable degree of short-run stabilization? Some critics suspect that to the extent that inflation-forecast targeting aims to serve as a monetary standard, it will inevitably be too rigid (for example, Friedman and Kuttner, 1996). Others argue that the attempt by inflation-forecast targeting central banks to leave themselves sufficient flexibility to pursue stabilization aims will inevitably undermine the credibility of their commitment to controlling inflation. To address this issue,

it is necessary to look more carefully at how inflation-forecast targeting is practiced – and at some of the variations that exist in current practice.

## Should Only the Inflation Forecast Matter?

Those central banks that have been most explicit about their use of a forecast-targeting procedure (with the exception of the Norges Bank, discussed below) have generally given primary emphasis to the way in which the inflation forecast for a particular future horizon determines the policy decision. This emphasis makes it clear why one speaks of "inflation-forecast targeting"; but is a single-minded focus on inflation an essential feature of the forecast-targeting approach?

As a logical matter, a forecast-targeting approach might involve any of a wide variety of types of target criteria. Nonetheless, there are compelling reasons to choose a criterion that implies a clear commitment to some particular inflation rate (on average) over the medium-to-long-term. The stabilization of inflation expectations offers clear benefits, some of which have been sketched above. Moreover, there is no good reason for the public's inflation expectations to remain anchored other than the existence of a credible commitment on the part of the central bank; for both economic theory and bitter experience teach that the inflation rate *can* vary widely and for long periods of time, depending on the nature of policy. In comparison to fluctuations in inflation, low-frequency movements in the real rate of economic growth are relatively modest and are less obviously dependent on monetary policy.

Some have suggested that if a central bank cares about the stability of the real economy as well as inflation – or if inflation forecast-targeting were to be adopted in countries like the United States, where the Federal Reserve Act assigns the Fed the mandate of promoting "maximum employment" as well as "stable prices" – then there should be an employment target (or growth target) as well as an inflation target. But even if an output or employment stabilization objective is assigned equal weight with inflation stabilization among the *goals* that a monetary policy is designed to serve, it does not follow that equal prominence should be given to *targets* for output or inflation under an ideal decision framework. If by a "target" one means a fixed numerical value of the variable that a central bank should always be aiming to achieve over some medium term, then an inflation target makes a great deal more sense than an employment target. In the case of inflation, monetary policy can achieve pretty much any long-run average rate that is desired. In the case of employment or real activity, monetary policy has short-run effects, but can have little effect on the average levels of such variables over longer periods; hence a fixed long-run target could be futile and in any event unnecessary (insofar as expectations regarding such variables ought not to be based on central bank pronouncements regarding targets).

But the argument that only inflation should have a numerical target does not mean that projections of real variables should not be taken into account in monetary policy decisions. In practice, the medium-run target for inflation does not suffice in itself to determine the appropriate current policy action, owing to the possibility of alternative transition paths by which that medium run might be reached. For example, a central bank facing high inflation might seek to return inflation to the target level more quickly following a disturbance, or more gradually. In choosing between these alternatives, it is reasonable to take into account the associated alternative paths of real variables

that can differ along the transition paths, even if monetary policy cannot affect the long-run levels of such variables.

Norway's Norges Bank has been the most explicit among current practitioners of inflation-forecast targeting about the way in which its target criterion involves real variables as well as inflation. Each issue of its *Monetary Policy Report* contains a box stating the criteria that the Bank looks for in an acceptable set of projections, described as the conditions that identify an appropriate policy intention – "an appropriate future interest rate path" (Norges Bank, *Monetary Policy Report* 2007/2, p. 12). The first criterion is that the inflation projection should show "inflation close to the target [of 2.5 percent per year] in the medium term"; but there is also a second criterion, which is that the projections "should provide a reasonable balance between the path for inflation and the path for capacity utilization." The two criteria are not intended as competing goals that must be balanced with one another; rather, the first indicates the situation that should eventually be reached (in a "medium term" that is not identified with a specific horizon), while the second describes the type of transition path by which it should be reached.

Short-term departures of the inflation rate from the medium-term target are justifiable to the extent that they are associated with a level of capacity utilization that is also temporarily different from its long-run level, in the direction such that faster convergence of inflation to the target rate would be possible only by keeping output away from potential to an even greater extent.[4] The Norges Bank checks whether its projections have this property by superimposing the inflation and output-gap projections in a single figure, like the one in *Figure 2*. This figure shows that in early 2007, Norway's inflation

---

[4] In past issues, the second criterion has stated even more explicitly that "the inflation gap [the departure of projected inflation from the medium-run target] and the output gap [the departure of projected output from potential] should be in reasonable proportion to each other until they close," and "should normally not be positive or negative at the same time further ahead" (Norges Bank, *Inflation Report* 2006/3, p. 10).

*Figure 2*

**The Norges Bank Target Criterion:
Proportionality between the Projected Inflation
Gap and Projected Output Gap**

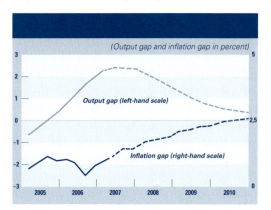

**Source:** This figure based on Chart 1.15 from the 2007/2 *Monetary Policy
Report* of the Norges Bank.

**Notes:** The dashed part of each line indicates projections for the next
three years under the Bank's baseline policy scenario. Each
*Monetary Policy Report* also includes a fan chart for each of
these variables (not shown here), as well as charts indicating
how the projections would be different under specific alternative
scenarios. The inflation gap plotted is for a consumer price index
(CPI) that is adjusted for tax changes and that excludes energy
prices.

rate was below the 2.5 percent target level, but
that at the same time, output was above potential.
The projections show that over the next three
years, with output above potential, inflation is
projected to rise, eventually approaching the
target rate, while at the same time the output
gap is projected to be closed at a similar rate.

Other forecast-targeting central banks have
been less willing to discuss openly the way in
which projections of output growth or other real
variables figure in their policy decisions, even

though it is fairly obvious that they do, to some
extent.[5] These banks make it clear that their
inflation targets, in their understanding, do
not require that inflation be projected to equal
the target rate except at horizons two or more
years into the future; but the banks are often
vague about the criteria used to select among
possible paths consistent with that medium-run
state.[6] This practice makes it appear as though
the inflation target alone determines the policy
decision. But other considerations are actually in
play, and explicit discussion of the criterion used
to select among transition paths would not only
increase the transparency of monetary policy,
but would also increase the credibility of the
central bank's commitment to its medium-run
target by making it easier for the public to judge
whether departures of the current inflation rate
from the target are consistent with a policy that
remains committed to that target.

## Is Forecast Targeting
## Intertemporally Consistent?

The degree to which publication of central
bank projections can be expected to shape the
expectations of private decisionmakers will
depend on how credible these projections are
as forecasts of the economy's likely evolution.
Among the possible grounds for doubt is a
tension inherent in the logic of the forecast-
targeting procedure itself. Production of
projections of the economy's evolution several
years into the future requires that the central
bank make assumptions about its conduct of
policy not merely in the immediate future,
but over the entire forecast horizon (and

---

[5] For example, in the overview at the beginning of each issue of the Bank of England's *Inflation Report*, the projection for GDP growth (reproduced
in *Figure 1A*) is always presented *first*, and only subsequently the projection for CPI inflation (*Figure 1B*), though the summary justification then
given for the most recent policy decision is much more explicit about how the inflation projection supports the decision. Proponents of inflation
targeting frequently stress that inflation-targeting central banks have in practice never been solely concerned with inflation (Bernanke, Laubach,
Mishkin, and Posen, 1999; King, 1999; Svensson, 1999). It is perhaps worth telling that in 2007 both the Norges Bank and Sweden's Riskbank
changed the names of their *Inflation Reports*, which are now instead called *Monetary Policy Reports*.

[6] In Svensson's (1997) theoretical argument for inflation targeting, the criterion that expected inflation two years in the future equal the target
rate suffices to determine the current interest rate decision completely, because in the simple model of that paper, interest rates have no effect
on inflation except with a two-year lag. This is not literally true, however, in the empirical models used for policy simulations in central banks.
The use of additional criteria by the Norges Bank, just discussed, makes it clear that there do remain additional degrees of freedom even after
convergence of the inflation projection to the target rate is required.

even beyond, in the case of a forward-looking model). But while the projections must specify policy far into the future each time they are produced, in each decision cycle policy is only *chosen* for a short period of time (say, for the coming month, after which there will be another decision).

Should this decision procedure be expected actually to produce the kind of future policy that is assumed in the projections? One might imagine, for example, a central bank wishing always to choose expansionary policy at the present moment, to keep employment high, while projecting that inflation will be reduced a year or two in the future, so that the expectation of disinflation will make it possible to have high employment with only moderate inflation. But if the procedure is one in which the disinflation is always promised two years in the future, private decisionmakers have no reason ever to expect any disinflation at all.

Thus one requirement for credibility of the central bank's projections is that the forecast-targeting procedure be *intertemporally consistent*; that is, the future policy that is assumed in the projections should coincide with the policy that the procedure itself can be expected to recommend, as long as those aspects of future conditions that are outside the control of the central bank turn out in the way that is currently anticipated. While this requirement may seem obvious, a number of apparently sensible approaches to forecast-targeting fail to satisfy it.

### Constant-Interest-Rate Projections

A popular approach in the early years of inflation-forecast targeting – used, for example, in the *Inflation Reports* of the Bank of England prior to August 2004 – was to construct projections

conditional upon a *constant interest rate* over the forecast horizon (Vickers, 1998; Jansson and Vredin, 2003). The appropriate current interest-rate decision was then taken to be the interest rate that, if expected to be maintained over the forecast horizon, would lead to projections satisfying the target criterion (for example, 2 percent inflation eight quarters in the future). This procedure had a number of advantages. First, a bank had only to consider variations in policy over a single dimension (alternative constant interest rates), with the consequence that a one-dimensional target criterion would suffice to identify the correct policy. Second, contemplated changes in the current interest-rate decision would be predicted to have nontrivial consequences, given that any change was expected (for purposes of the projection exercise) to be a permanent change. Finally, it was possible to construct projections without the bank's having to tip its hand as to the likely character of future policy.

But constant-interest-rate projections raise a number of conceptual problems (Goodhart, 2001; Honkapohja and Mitra, 2005; Leitemo, 2003; Woodford, 2005). The assumption that the nominal interest rate will remain fixed at some level, regardless of how inflation or other variables may evolve, is not sensible. Moreover, in forward-looking (rational expectations) models of the kind that are now beginning to be used by central banks, the assumption of a constant nominal interest rate often implies an indeterminate price level, so that it becomes impossible to solve uniquely for an inflation forecast under any such interest-rate assumption.[7] In models with backward-looking expectations, the model can be solved, but such policies often imply explosive inflation dynamics.[8] Such difficulties appear to have been a frequent problem with the constant-interest-rate projections of the Bank of

---

[7] This was the basis of the critique of interest rate rules by Sargent and Wallace (1975). For discussion of how such policies lead to indeterminacy in modern micro-founded "New-Keynesian" models, see Woodford (2003, chap. 4).

[8] This was the basis of the critique of an interest-rate pegging policy by Friedman (1968); the idea goes back to Wicksell's (1898) analysis of the "cumulative process" of inflation under an interest rate policy.

*Figure 3*

**A Constant-Interest-Rate Projection Compared with a Projection Based on Market Expectations of Interest Rates**

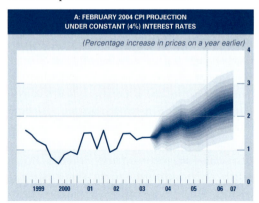

**Source:** Bank of England *Inflation Report*, August 2004.

England (Goodhart, 2001), which often showed the inflation rate *passing through* the target rate at the eight-quarter horizon, but not *converging* to it. *Figure 3A* provides an example. In such a case, it is not obvious why anyone should believe this policy is consistent with the inflation target, or expect that inflation expectations should be anchored as a result of a commitment to such a policy.

The most fundamental problem, however, is there will often be no reason to expect interest rates to remain constant over the policy horizon. Indeed, constant-interest-rate projections themselves often imply that the people making the projections should *not* expect the interest rate to be maintained over the forecast horizon. Consider, for example, the inflation projection shown in *Figure 3A*, a constant-interest-rate projection on the basis of which the February 2004 Bank of England *Inflation Report* concluded that a 4 percent policy rate was appropriate at that time.[9] The figure shows that under the assumption of a constant 4 percent policy rate, consumer price inflation

was projected (under the most likely evolution, indicated by the darkest area) to pass through the target rate of 2.0 percent at the eight-quarter horizon (indicated by the vertical dashed line), and then to continue rising in the following year. Thus, if the policy rate were to be held at 4 percent for a year, the Bank's expectation in February 2004 should have been (under the most likely evolution, given what was known then) that in February 2005 a similar exercise would forecast consumer price inflation to pass through 2.0 percent at the *one*-year horizon, and to exceed 2.0 percent during the *second* year. Hence, the bank has essentially forecasted that in a year's time, under the most likely evolution, the policy committee would have reason to raise the policy rate. To put it another way, the February 2004 projection itself could have been taken as evidence that the Bank should *not* have expected the policy rate to remain at 4 percent over the following eight quarters.

As these issues have come to be understood, a number of central banks that formerly relied upon constant-interest-rate projections (such

---

[9] By the "policy rate," I mean the Bank's target for overnight rates in the pound sterling money markets, which it seeks to maintain through its various operations. This is currently called the "official Bank Rate"; it is essentially the equivalent of the Federal Funds Rate operating target in the case of the Fed.

as the Bank of England since August 2004 and the Swedish Riksbank until earlier this year) have switched to an alternative approach; this is the construction of projections based on *market expectations* of the future path of short-term interest rates, as inferred from the term structure of interest rates and/or futures markets. The use of projections based on market expectations allows a central bank to avoid assuming a constant interest rate when there are clear reasons to expect interest rates to change soon, while still not expressing any view of its own about the likely future path of interest rates. In the case just discussed, market expectations were for the policy rate to rise later in the year (as in fact it did), and consequently the Bank of England's February 2004 market-expectations projection shown in *Figure 3B* implied a less rapid increase in the inflation rate, and consumer price inflation only around 2.0 percent three years in the future.

But the market expectations approach does not ultimately answer the objections just raised to constant-interest-rate projections (Goodhart, 2005; Woodford, 2005). If one simply feeds into a macroeconomic model a specific path for the short-term nominal interest rate that is apparently expected by the markets, it is highly problematic to assume that this interest rate path exists *regardless* of how inflation and other variables evolve. Again, such an assumption will imply indeterminacy in the case of a forward-looking model, and unstable inflation dynamics in the case of a backward-looking model; for these problems arise not from the assumption of a *constant* interest rate, but from the assumption of an *exogenously specified* interest rate, unaffected by the evolution of endogenous variables such as inflation or central bank policy.

An even more fundamental problem is that market expectations can identify only a single candidate assumption about future policy to consider. If the projections based on this

particular assumption do not satisfy the target criterion, what alternative policy should one consider instead? One needs a principle for finding a suitable policy assumption other than the mere fact that it is expected by the markets, and hence the issue of intertemporal consistency must be faced.

**Choosing a Policy Path**

An alternative approach to forecast-targeting uses projections based on the central bank's own forecast of its likely future policy. In the case of both the Norges Bank (since 2005) and the Riksbank (since the beginning of 2007), each issue of the *Monetary Policy Report* now includes a "fan chart" for the evolution of the policy rate, alongside the similar charts for inflation and output. These often do not indicate an expectation that the policy rate will remain constant.

In the approach now used by these two banks, it is necessary in each decision cycle to contemplate alternative *paths* for policy, and not simply alternative choices for the current interest-rate target. The policy path that is chosen is one that is found to result in projections that are desirable from the standpoint of certain criteria. The Norges Bank is fairly explicit about these criteria; this is the significance of the list of "Criteria for an appropriate interest-rate path" in its *Monetary Policy Report*, mentioned earlier. The Riksbank describes the decision as simply reflecting the preferences of the Executive Board over alternative possible projected outcomes (Sveriges Riksbank, *Monetary Policy Report* 2007/1, p. 20). While in each case a choice is effectively made over paths, both central banks emphasize that the published interest-rate paths under their "baseline scenarios" are to be understood as forecasts rather than as *commitments*. The exercise of choosing a path is repeated anew in each decision cycle, and in each case it is only the choice of the level of interest rates in the immediate future that has implications for policy actions.

The question of the intertemporal consistency of such a procedure therefore remains. In fact, the approach of selecting among alternative paths for policy through a vote of the Executive Board is unlikely to result in intertemporally consistent choices, and for reasons unrelated to any incoherence of preferences or failure to optimize correctly by that body. Even in the case of a single decisionmaker who minimizes a well-defined loss function that remains the same over time, using a correct economic model that also remains the same over time, and who never makes any calculation errors, the choice of a new optimal path for policy each period will not lead to intertemporal consistency. For in the case of a forward-looking model of the transmission mechanism, the procedure will lead to the choice of a forward path for policy that this same procedure will *not* lead the decisionmaker to continue in subsequent decision cycles, even if there have been no unexpected developments in the meantime, as explained in Woodford (1999). The reason is the same as in the celebrated critique of discretionary monetary policy by Kydland and Prescott (1977): Before making a policy decision, the monetary authority prefers a forward path in which policy is expected to be tight, because of the benefits of low inflation expectations; but after making that decision, a looser policy is preferred, because the inflationary expectations can no longer be affected by the policy that is actually chosen (as opposed to the policy that was anticipated).

Intertemporal consistency can instead be maintained if the path of policy is chosen so that the projections satisfy not a point-in-time target criterion (say, a criterion relating only to projections eight quarters in the future) but rather a *sequence* of target criteria, each taking the same form, but for a sequence of horizons progressively farther in the future. Suppose that, in the spirit of the criterion illustrated in *Figure 2*,

the policy path is chosen so that the projected inflation gap is proportional to the projected output gap (but with an opposite sign), at *every* future date [10] – both in the near term, when both gaps may be substantially different from zero, and in the longer term, when (in order to satisfy the criterion) both will have to approach zero. Then according to such projections, if the economy evolves as anticipated, at a later date (say, a year from now) the same procedure should result in choosing to continue the policy path that is chosen now, as the continuation path should lead to projections which continue to satisfy the target criterion at all horizons.

The target criterion can be chosen to reflect a quest for balance among competing stabilization objectives. Indeed, one of the advantages of commitment to a target criterion of the kind just discussed is that it allows the central bank to make clear its commitment to a "dual mandate" (the target criterion used to evaluate both the short-term and long-term projections treats the inflation gap and the output gap *symmetrically*) while nonetheless making constantly visible the bank's expectation that inflation should return to a fixed target value in the medium term. (Acceptable projections would always have the latter property, but as an implication of the bank's *economic model*, rather than any lexicographic priority of inflation stabilization among its *objectives*.)

In the case of a sufficiently simple model of the monetary transmission mechanism, it is possible to choose a target criterion of this form that implements an optimal state-contingent policy; the sequential target criterion essentially corresponds to a sequence of first-order conditions for dynamic optimization under commitment. Svensson and Woodford (2005) and Giannoni and Woodford (2005) illustrate this for a variety of simple models that incorporate important features of current-

---

[10] More precisely, the criterion should be satisfied at each date after the shortest horizon at which it is still possible for a change in monetary policy to affect the projected evolution of these variables.

generation empirical "New-Keynesian" models. In practice, however, a fully optimal target criterion is likely to be too complex for use in explaining policy decisions to the public. It makes more sense to choose a simple criterion that incorporates relatively robust features of desirable policies. One such example of a robust principle of optimal policy is the rule that higher projected inflation should be accepted when associated with a projected movement to a more negative output gap. Another is the principle that departures of the overall inflation rate from the long-run inflation target should be allowed in connection with adjustments of the structure of relative prices, but should not persist longer than is required for the adjustment of relative prices to occur. Thus it is desirable to allow CPI inflation to increase in response to an increase in the real price of energy, as this allows greater stability of the rate of growth of nonenergy prices; but the increase in CPI inflation should not be greater, or last longer, than can be justified on that ground. While the exact quantitative specification of the target criterion that is optimal depends on details of one's model, a target criterion that incorporates these qualitative features is likely to approximate optimal policy reasonably well.

### Are Economic Forecasts Accurate Enough to be Reliable for Inflation-Forecast Targeting?

An obvious worry about inflation-forecast targeting is that policy decisions may depend on inaccurate forecasts. Indeed, systematic biases in the central bank's forecasting model might even lead to systematic biases in policy. For example, even if a central bank *aims* consistently at a low rate of inflation, its policy might in fact generate higher inflation year after year, if the bank uses a model that forecasts inflation lower on average than what actually occurs.

*Figure 4*

**Real-time Estimates of the U.S. Output Gap Compared to "Final" Estimates by the Fed Staff as of 1994**

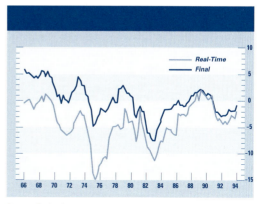

**Source:** Orphanides (2003).

One obvious reason why there might well be forecast errors with the same sign for many years arises from mistakes in real-time estimation of productivity trends, which could cause estimates of the output gap to be high or low. *Figure 4*, taken from Orphanides (2003), illustrates this danger by comparing the real-time estimates of the output gap available to the Fed throughout the 1970s and 1980s to its estimates in 1994 of what the output gap had actually been in each quarter. Of course, the 1970s experienced a productivity slowdown, which was not fully recognized at the time. Thus, in the 1970s, the Federal Reserve believed that the output gap was negative for the entire decade, with the economy more than 5 percent below potential GDP for years at a time, and as much as 15 percent below potential GDP in early 1975. But by 1994, when the productivity slowdown had been recognized, the Federal Reserve came to believe that the output gap during the 1970s had instead been positive except during the slump period of 1974–76, and never below 5 percent of potential even then. This kind of mistake could easily lead to monetary policy with an unintended but systematic inflationary bias for years in a row, and Orphanides argues that this pattern explains the "Great Inflation" of the 1970s.

While real-time estimation of productivity trends remains a difficult problem for central banks, I do not feel that this is a sufficient reason to abandon forecast-based policy, or even to insist upon a target criterion that does not involve the output gap. The optimal policy at a given point in time inevitably depends on whatis expected to occur later, not only because present actions have delayed effects, but also because the more immediate effects of policy actions depend on what they are taken to signal about future policy. Hence a policy rule that always prescribes the same response to current conditions, taking no account of what may already be foreseeable about future conditions, will be inferior to one that makes appropriate use of whatever information is available about the future. Forecast-targeting procedures are a natural way of making use of such information so as to achieve a desirable outcome in any of a wide range of possible situations. Svensson and Woodford (2005) discuss in detail the advantages of forecast-targeting procedures as a way of implementing a dynamically optimal state-contingent policy.

Similarly, standard economic models imply that the gap between actual output and the economy's potential is relevant to judging the welfare consequences of alternative monetary policies. Moreover, target criteria that relate inflation measures to an appropriately defined output gap provide characterizations of optimal policy that are especially robust, in the sense of remaining valid in the case of a large number of different types of possible disturbances.[11] If a measure of the output gap is known to be imprecise, the likely degree of imprecision should be taken into account when judging whether there is a basis for accepting a projected near-term inflation rate different from the long-run target. But to a first approximation, an appropriate response is *not* to change the weight placed on one's estimate of the output gap in the target criterion; instead, one need only take care to use an optimal *estimate* of the output gap when checking the target criterion, which adjusts the size of the output estimate for the level of certainty about it (Svensson and Woodford, 2003). For example, if one has little useful evidence about the output gap, the optimal estimate will seldom depart from the unconditional mean of zero, and so the inclusion of an output-gap correction in the target criterion will be of no import; but if one can be fairly sure of the sign of the gap, at least sometimes, it will be appropriate to take this information into account.

Of course, even the best possible forecasts will nonetheless often be inaccurate. The key to avoiding the possibility of an entire decade of inflation well above the target level, due to systematic bias in the underlying model, is to make a commitment to correct past target misses. That is, a year or two of inflation higher than desired should result in policy that deliberately aims at an inflation rate *lower* than the long-run inflation target for the next few years — to correct the overshoot. In this way, even if the central bank uses a model that produces a downward-biased forecast of inflation for many years in a row (due, for example, to a productivity slowdown that leads to a persistent overestimate of potential output), it will not allow excess inflation to occur for very long before policy is tightened.

One way to institutionalize this kind of error-correction would be through commitment to a target path for the *price level*, and not just a target annual inflation rate. Of course, in such a setting, temporary departures from the price-level target path should be allowed in proportion to the output gap. However, target misses —

---

[11] Giannoni and Woodford (2005) derive robustly optimal target criteria for a range of alternative New-Keynesian models, and all are "output-gap-adjusted inflation targets" broadly similar to the criterion illustrated in *Figure 2*.

that is, departures of the output-gap-adjusted price level from the target path – would then require a policy under which the gap between the adjusted price level and the deterministic trend path would be projected to be eliminated at a certain constant rate. If the required rate of error-correction was quite slow, such a criterion could justify a *price level* persistently above the target path, but not higher by a growing rate (unless the overestimate of potential output were itself to grow steadily as well).

A commitment to error-correction has even greater advantages if one supposes that the private sector should have a better real-time estimate of productivity than the central bank. In this case, even if the central bank overestimates potential output and accordingly pursues too expansionary a policy, the private-sector recognition of this pattern will lead to anticipation of the subsequent disinflationary correction, restraining wage and price increases. Thus, as pointed out by Gorodnichenko and Shapiro (2006), under price-level targeting, mistakes in the central bank's real-time estimates of potential output have less of an effect on inflation outcomes – even in the short-run, and not just over longer periods of time. They argue that Fed policy under Alan Greenspan incorporated elements of error-correction and propose that this is why uncertainty about the productivity trend in the late 1990s was so much less of a problem than in the 1970s. Aoki and Nikolov (2005) similarly find that coefficient errors in the central bank's model of the economy result in less deterioration of economic performance in the case of a forecast-targeting procedure with an output-gap-adjusted price-level target than in the case of a gap-adjusted inflation target.

## Forecast Targeting in the United States: An Idea Whose Time Has Come

Forecast targeting offers great promise as an approach to the conduct of monetary policy. If properly executed, it can serve to anchor expectations about the future value of a currency – the traditional aim of a monetary standard – while still allowing substantial attention to short-run stabilization concerns. But the realization of this promise requires that the right version of forecast targeting be adopted.

Specifically, forecast-targeting central banks must learn to be more explicit about the near-term target criteria that their projections are expected to satisfy, rather than speaking only about their medium-run targets for inflation. The forecast-targeting exercise is only internally consistent – and therefore able to serve as effective means of communication with sophisticated observers – if the assumptions made about the bank's own future policy are chosen appropriately. Finally, given the inevitable limitations of both the information and the economic models available to central banks, the target criteria should incorporate some degree of commitment to error-correction, rather than being purely forward-looking. Approaches that address these concerns are available in principle, and central banks around the world are making steady progress at the refinement of methods of analysis and communication that can achieve these ambitious goals in practice.

Would a forecast-targeting approach make sense for the U.S. Federal Reserve? Quantitative projections already play an important role in the internal deliberations of the Federal Open Market Committee (FOMC). Ben Bernanke, the current chairman of the Fed, devoted a speech in 2004 (when serving as a member of the Board of Governors) to what he called "forecast-based policy" and asserted that while there was no exclusive commitment to such an approach, "the Federal Reserve relies primarily on the forecast-based approach for making policy." But full implementation of a forecast-targeting approach of the kind discussed above would require two important further steps: Adoption of an explicit target criterion that would provide a structure for policy deliberations, and public discussion of the projections as a central element in the Fed's communication policy.

Both steps are actively under consideration at the Fed, though no such innovations will be undertaken without thorough discussion. The minutes of the FOMC meeting of March 20–21, 2007, indicate that, as at several other meetings over the past year, the Committee discussed both "the possible advantages and disadvantages of specifying a numerical price objective for monetary policy" and the possibility of "an enhanced role for projections in explaining policy."

In my view, both steps would have important advantages. While the Fed's existing procedures have been quite successful at maintaining a low and stable rate of inflation over the past two decades, improving the degree to which medium-run inflation expectations in the United States are anchored remains an important concern for the Fed. The Fed's concern in late 2002 and early 2003 that deflationary expectations could develop represents one recent instance in which weaknesses of the current approach have been apparent; more recent fears that undue expectations of continuing inflation could be created by relatively transitory increases in commodity-price inflation provide another. The Fed has found it necessary both to give more explicit signals as to the likely forward path of monetary policy and to talk more about its own projections regarding future inflation. Such communication would be both less ambiguous and more credible in the context of an explicit forecast-targeting strategy.

Proposals that the Fed adopt some form of inflation targeting often meet with the objection that this would require legislative authorization. (The minutes of the FOMC discussion just cited are careful to state that "participants emphasized that any such move would need to be consistent with the Committee's statutory objectives for promoting maximum employment as well as price stability.") But as I have argued above, a forecast-targeting approach does not require that a central bank close its eyes to the consequences of its policies for employment. The projections that are considered in policy deliberations should include projections for real variables, and indeed a sensible target criterion should involve these projections as much as the projection for inflation.

A forecast-targeting procedure similar to that of the Norges Bank could plausibly be introduced as a framework intended to ensure that policy conforms to the mandates of the Federal Reserve Act and to make this conformity more evident to Congress and to the public. Rather than a further arrogation of power to the Fed to define its own objectives, adoption of forecast targeting would represent a voluntary decision by the Fed to make itself more accountable. In addition to increasing the effectiveness of the Fed's communication, such a step would help to reconcile the Fed's operational independence with democratic principles.

The conduct of monetary policy under a forecast-targeting framework would probably not have been greatly different than the policy that the Fed has followed in recent years. But in the absence of a clearer commitment to a systematic framework for the conduct of policy, the public has little ground for confidence that the stability achieved over the past decade has not simply been due to luck or the personalities of particular members of the Federal Open Market Committee, so that the situation could change at any time. Adoption of an explicit forecast-targeting framework would instead allow confidence in the value of the dollar to be maintained in the face of changing circumstances and facilitate continued stabilization of the real economy as well. It is time for the Federal Reserve to build on the experience of other central banks and develop a forecast-targeting framework suited to its own policy commitments and institutional setting.

*I would like to thank Olivier Blanchard, Rick Mishkin, Julio Rotemberg, Argia Sbordone, Lars Svensson, and the editors of JEP for helpful comments on an earlier draft.*

## REFERENCES

**Aoki, K., and N. Kalin.** 2005. "Rule-Based Monetary Policy under Central Bank Learning." Center for Economic Policy Research Discussion Paper 5056.

**Bank of England.** Various years. *Inflation Report*, various issues.

**Benati, L.** 2006. "UK Monetary Regimes and Macroeconomic Stylized Facts." Bank of England Working Paper 290.

**Bernanke, B. S.** 2004. "The Logic of Monetary Policy." Speech before the National Economists Club, December 2, 2004, Washington, D.C.

**Bernanke, B. S., T. Laubach, F. S. Mishkin, and A. S. Posen.** 1999. *Inflation Targeting: Lessons from the International Experience.* Princeton, NJ: Princeton University Press.

**Estrella, A., and F. S. Mishkin.** 1997. "Is There a Role for Monetary Aggregates in the Conduct of Monetary Policy?" *Journal of Monetary Economics*, 40(2): 279–304.

**Fischer, B., M. Lenza, H. Pill, and L. Reichlin.** 2006. "Money and Monetary Policy: The ECB Experience 1999 –2006." http://www.ecb.int/events/pdf/conferences/cbc4/ReichlinPillLenzaFisher.pdf.

**Friedman, B. M., and K. N. Kuttner.** 1996. "A Price Target for U.S. Monetary Policy? Lessons from the Experience with Money Growth Targets." *Brookings Papers on Economic Activity*, 1996(1): 77–125, 144–46.

**Friedman, M.** 1968. "The Role of Monetary Policy." *American Economic Review*, 58(1): 1–17.

**Giannoni, M. P., and M. Woodford.** 2005. "Optimal Inflation Targeting Rules." In *The Inflation Targeting Debate*, ed. B. S. Bernanke and M. Woodford, chap. 3. Chicago: University of Chicago Press.

**Goodhart, C. A. E.** 2001. "Monetary Transmission Lags and the Formulation of the Policy Decision on Interest Rates." Federal Reserve Bank of St. Louis Review, July/August 2001, 165–81.

**Goodhart, C. A. E.** 2005. "The Interest Rate Conditioning Assumption." Financial Markets Group Discussion Paper 547.

**Gorodnichenko, Y., and M. D. Shapiro.** 2006. "Monetary Policy When Potential Output is Uncertain: Understanding the Growth Gamble of the 1990s." National Bureau of Economic Research Working Paper 12268.

**Honkapohja, S., and K. Mitra.** 2005. "Performance of Inflation Targeting Based on Constant Interest Rate Projections." *Journal of Economic Dynamics and Control*, 29(11): 1867–92.

**Jansson, P., and A. Vredin.** 2003. "Forecast-Based Monetary Policy: The Case of Sweden." *International Finance*, 6(3): 349–80.

King, M. 1999. "Challenges for Monetary Policy: New and Old." In *New Challenges for Monetary Policy*, 11–58. Kansas City: Federal Reserve Bank of Kansas City.

King, M. 2005. "What Has Inflation Targeting Achieved?" In *The Inflation Targeting Debate*, ed. B. S. Bernanke and M. Woodford, chap. 1. Chicago: University of Chicago Press.

Kydland, F. E., and E. C. Prescott. 1977. "Rules Rather than Discretion: The Inconsistency of Optimal Plans." *Journal of Political Economy*, 85(3): 473–91.

Leitemo, K. 2003. "Targeting Inflation by Constant-Interest-Rate Forecasts." *Journal of Money, Credit and Banking*, 35(4): 609–26.

Norges Bank. Various years. *Inflation Report* and Monetary Policy Report, various issues. (In 2007 the Norges Bank changed the name of its *Inflation Reports*; they are now called *Monetary Policy Reports*.)

Orphanides, A. 2003. "The Quest for Prosperity without Inflation." *Journal of Monetary Economics*, 50(3): 633–63.

Sargent, T. J., and N. Wallace. 1975. "Rational Expectations, the Optimal Monetary Instrument and the Optimal Money Supply Rule." *Journal of Political Economy*, 83(2): 241–54.

Svensson, L. E. O. 1997. "Inflation Forecast Targeting: Implementing and Monitoring Inflation Targeting." *European Economic Review*, 41(6): 1111–46.

Svensson, L. E. O. 1999. "Inflation Targeting as a Monetary Policy Rule." *Journal of Monetary Economics*, 43(3): 607–54.

Svensson, L. E. O., and M. Woodford. 2003. "Indicator Variables for Optimal Policy." *Journal of Monetary Economics*, 50(3): 691–720.

Svensson, L. E. O., and M. Woodford. 2005. "Implementing Optimal Policy through Inflation-Forecast Targeting." In *The Inflation Targeting Debate*, ed. B.S. Bernanke and M. Woodford, chap. 2. Chicago: University of Chicago Press.

Sveriges Riksbank. Various years. Inflation Policy Report and Monetary Policy Report, various issues. (In 2007 Sweden's Riskbank changed the name of its *Inflation Reports*; they are now called *Monetary Policy Reports*.)

Taylor, J. B. 1993. "Discretion Versus Policy Rules in Practice." *Carnegie-Rochester Conference Series on Public Policy*, 39(1): 195–214.

Vickers, J. 1998. "Inflation Targeting in Practice: The U.K. Experience." Bank of England Quarterly Bulletin, November.

Wicksell, K. 1898. *Interest and Prices.* (English translation by R.F. Kahn, London: Macmillan, 1936).

Woodford, M. 1999. "Commentary: How Should Monetary Policy Be Conducted in an Era of Price Stability?" In *New Challenges for Monetary Policy*, 277–316. Kansas City: Federal Reserve Bank of Kansas City.

Woodford, M. 2004. "Inflation Targeting and Optimal Monetary Policy." Federal Reserve Bank of St. Louis Economic Review, July/August, 2004, 15–41.

Woodford, M. 2003. *Interest and Prices: Foundations of a Theory of Monetary Policy.* Princeton, NJ: Princeton University Press.

Woodford, M. 2005. "Central-Bank Communication and Policy Effectiveness." In *The Greenspan Era: Lessons for the Future*, 399–474. Kansas City: Federal Reserve Bank of Kansas City.

# INCORPORATING CONJUNCTURAL ANALYSIS IN STRUCTURAL MODELS*

Domenico Giannone (European Central Bank, ECARES and CEPR)
Francesca Monti (ECARES and Université Libre de Bruxelles)
Lucrezia Reichlin (London Business School and CEPR)

## Introduction

This volume celebrates the work of Michael Woodford and his many contributions to economics.

One of Mike's most influential papers is the 1997 paper (co-authored with Julio Rotemberg) "An optimization-based econometric framework for the evaluation of monetary policy." This paper constituted the first attempt at estimation of a small scale dynamic stochastic general equilibrium model (DSGE) in which prices are set by monopolistically competitive firms, and prices cannot be instantaneously and costlessly adjusted. Since the work of Rotemberg and Woodford, these models have become more complex and increasingly large [see Christiano, Eichenbaum and Evans (2005), Smets and Wouters (2003), and, more recently, Christoffel, Coenen and Warne (2008) and Adolfson, Laséen, Lindé and Svensson (2008)]. By explicitly taking into account forward-

looking behavior on the part of the agents, DSGEs provide a useful framework to analyze the effects of alternative policies. These models are now routinely used in many central banks, including the European Central Bank, and knowledge has been built up on their reliability, their forecasting performance and on what are the reasonable values for calibrated parameters and the setting of the priors.

One of the limitations of these tools is that they are not suitable for policy analysis in real time since they do not take advantage of the information contained in higher frequency (and hence more timely) data releases in order to now-cast and forecast the key variables in the model. For the practical use of these models in policy institutions this is an important problem given the publication lag of many key quarterly variables. For example, in the U.S., the first official figure for GDP is the preliminary estimate published at the end of the month following the end of the reference quarter. In

* The authors are grateful to Gunter Coenen, Chris Sims, Argia Sbordone and all the seminar participants at the Federal Reserve Bank of NY (March 2008), the Working Group on Forecasting of the European System of Central Banks Meeting (2008), the EABCN conference on "Using Euro Area Data: Issues and Consequences for Economic Analysis" (March 2008), the Bank of Italy conference on "DSGE in the policy environment" (June 2008), the Bank of England (September 2008) and EUROSTAT (September 2008) for useful comments and suggestions.

the Euro Area, the first official figure is the flash estimate which is published about six weeks after the end of the reference quarter.

Monthly timely indicators such as surveys, car registrations and other variables used in conjunctural analysis, are typically not the focus of structural analysis. The analysis of this information is performed by short-term forecasters and it is based on either judgement or reduced form models. Usual practice for the structural modelers is to take the early estimates produced by the forecasters and use them as if they were observations as an input in the model. However, treating forecasts as observations, albeit noisy, assigns to the conjunctural analysts a knowledge of the future that is totally unrealistic. It would be like saying that they *see* into the future with some noise, rather than forecasting future economic conditions with their current information set.

In our contribution to this volume we will present new ideas aiming at adapting the DSGE framework for the purpose of real time analysis. We draw from Giannone, Monti and Reichlin (2008) and present a framework to combine a reduced form statistical model used to bridge staggered monthly releases and quarterly GDP with a structural DSGE model. In the example we present here, the statistical model is the one developed by Giannone, Reichlin and Small (2008) and widely used in central banks, while the DSGE is a prototypical New-Keynesian model as the one in Del Negro and Schorfheide (2004). In Giannone, Monti and Reichlin (2008), we illustrate a more general framework, based on the same ideas.

Our framework allows us to update the forecast at the time of each data release and monitor in real time key quantities, both observable variables like GDP and unobservable, model-based variables, such as total factor productivity (TFP) or the output gap.

In our approach, we will take the estimated quarterly DSGE model at face value and keep the estimated parameters as they are produced by the quarterly DSGE modelers. To exploit monthly information in a model consistent way, we derive the monthly state space representation that corresponds to the quarterly model and augment it with additional series which are believed to provide early information on the key quarterly variables of the model which are published late. On the basis of this framework, we can update the now-cast and forecast of the key quarterly variables taking into account the real time data flow. That is, we can update the estimates each time new data is released throughout the quarter. This allows us to interpret the early releases with the lenses of the model. By combining structural analysis with conjunctural analysis we can update our "stories", in principle, each day of the month. An additional interesting feature of the model is that we can assess the marginal impact of particular news on the variables of interest.

A key feature of our methodology is that the extra information provided by the monthly panel is valuable only because it is more timely. At the end of the quarter, the DSGE combined with the statistical model for monthly variables and the quarterly DSGE model with no extra information produce the same results.

The method of this chapter is related to other approaches that combine reduced form and structural analysis, but differs both in techniques and objectives. Del Negro et al. (2007) have proposed a framework which combines VAR and DSGE analysis to provide the modeler with a tool for attributing the desired weight to the structural model with respect to the VAR via a prior. Boivin and Giannoni (2006), on the other hand, use information in large panels of data to obtain better estimates of the states of the structural model in a framework in which the variables of interest are observed with an error. While their aim is to improve on the estimation of the quarterly DSGE model, we choose not to interfere with the estimation of the model's parameters. At the end of the quarter, our augmented model is the same as the structural quarterly DSGE.

The paper is organized as follows. First, we explain the methodology. Second, we illustrate the design of the empirical application based on the New-Keynesian model of Del Negro and Schorfheide (2004) and a panel of thirteen monthly series for the U.S. economy. Third, we describe the design of the forecast exercise and discuss the empirical results. The last section concludes.

## The Methodology

We consider structural quarterly models whose log-linearized solution have the form:

$$s_{t_q} = T_\theta s_{t_q - 1} + B_\theta \varepsilon_{t_q}, \qquad (1)$$

$$Y_{t_q} = M_\theta(L) s_{t_q},$$

where $t_q$ is time in quarters, $Y_{t_q} = (y_{1,t_q}, ..., y_{k,t_q})'$ is a set of observable variables which are transformed to be stationary, $s_{t_q}$ are the states of the model and $\varepsilon_{t_q}$ are structural orthonormal shocks. The filter $M_\theta(L) = M_{0,\theta} + M_{1,\theta}L + ... + M_{p,\theta}L^p$, the autoregressive matrix $T_\theta$ and the coefficients $B_\theta$ are function of the deep, behavioral parameters which are collected in the vector $\theta$. We will consider the model and the parameters as given by the structural modeler who obtained them by estimation or calibration.

As it is standard, we consider the situation in which the model is estimated at the quarterly frequency and the variables are key quarterly series, such as GDP and national accounts data, or variables that are available at higher frequencies, like financial or price data, but enter the model as quarterly, either as averages

over the quarter or as end of the quarter values.

In this standard case, the model can be updated only when the quarterly observations become available: Therefore one must wait for the end of the quarter or even later, when the variables that are published the latest are finally released. Notice that in a quarterly model also variables with monthly or higher native frequency are incorporated with a delay when they enter the model.

Our objective is to define a framework in which the statistical model used to exploit monthly data releases, either referring to variables included in the model as quarterly or to variables that can provide early information about GDP or other key quantities, can be linked in a consistent way to the structural model so as to obtain early estimates of the variables considered by the model.

The statistical model we will use is that developed by Giannone, Reichlin and Small (2008). This is a model that aims at bridging the monthly information as it becomes available throughout the quarter with quarterly quantities. The interesting feature of the model is that it can incorporate information contained in many monthly data and it provides consistent estimates from panels of data with jagged edge, that is data that, due to publication lags, have missing information at the end of the sample. In what follows, we will show how to link this statistical framework with the structural model.

Let us define by $t_m$ the time in months and denote by $Y_{t_m} = (y_{1,t_m}, ..., y_{k,t_m})'$ the vector of possible latent monthly counterparts of the variables that enter the quarterly model. These variables are transformed so as to correspond to a quarterly quantity when observed at the last month of each quarter, i.e. when $t_m$ corresponds to March, June, September or December.

For example let $y_{i,t_q}$ be the CPI inflation ($\pi_{t_q} = (\log P_{t_q} - \log P_{t_q-1}) \times 100$) and suppose that it enters the models as average over the quarter, then:

$$
\begin{aligned}
y_{i,t_m} &= [(\log P_{t_m} + \log P_{t_m-1} + \log P_{t_m-2}) \\
&\quad - (\log P_{t_m-3} + \log P_{t_m-4} \\
&\quad + \log P_{t_m-5})] \times 100 \\
&\approx [\log (P_{t_m} + P_{t_m-1} + P_{t_m-2}) \\
&\quad - \log (P_{t_m-3} + \log P_{t_m-4} \\
&\quad + \log P_{t_m-5})] \times 100.
\end{aligned}
$$

Let us further consider additional monthly variables that carry information on current economic conditions. We define by $X_{t_m} = (x_{1,t}, \ldots, x_{n,t})'$ the vector of these auxiliary stationary monthly variables transformed as above so as to correspond to quarterly quantities at the end of each quarter.

For example, let us consider the index of capacity utilization $CU_{t_m}$ and suppose that, to make it stationary, we have to take first differences. Then, assuming $CU_{t_m}$ is in the $j$-th position of the vector of auxiliary variables, we have:

$$
x_{j,t_m} = \frac{1}{3}[(CU_{t_m} + CU_{t_m-1} + CU_{t_m-2}) -
$$

$$
(CU_{t_m-3} + CU_{t_m-4} + CU_{t_m-5})],
$$

which, when observed at the last month of a quarter, corresponds to the quarterly change of the average capacity utilization over that quarter.[1]

Let us first consider for simplicity how to incorporate the monthly information contained in $Y_{t_m}$. We cannot use directly the model since the latter specifies the dynamics of the data at a quarterly frequency, hence we need to define a monthly dynamics that is compatible with the model.

In accordance with our definition of the monthly variables, we can define the vector of monthly states $s_{t_m}$ as a set of latent variables which corresponds to its quarterly model-based concept when observed at the last month of each quarter. Hence, it follows that our original state equation:

$$
s_{t_q} = T_\theta \, s_{t_q-1} + B_\theta \varepsilon_{t_q},
$$

can be rewritten in terms of the monthly latent states as:

$$
s_{t_m} = T_\theta \, s_{t_m-3} + B_\theta \varepsilon_{t_m},
$$

when $t_m$ corresponds to the last month of a quarter.

We will assume that the monthly states follow a VAR(1). Hence:

$$
s_{t_m} = T_m \, s_{t_m-1} + B_m \varepsilon_{m,t_m}, \tag{2}
$$

where $\varepsilon_{m,t_m}$ are orthonormal shocks. This implies:

$$
\begin{aligned}
s_{t_m} &= T_m^3 \, s_{t_m-3} + T_m^2 B_m \, \varepsilon_{m,t_m-2} \\
&\quad + T_m B_m \varepsilon_{m,t_m-1} + B_m \varepsilon_{m,t_m}.
\end{aligned}
$$

This last equation gives us a unique mapping from the coefficients of the quarterly model to the coefficients of the monthly model, which can be recovered from the following equations:

$$
\begin{aligned}
T_m &= T_\theta^{\frac{1}{3}}, \\
\text{vec}(B_m B_m') &= (I + T_m \otimes T_m + T_m^2 \otimes T_m^2)^{-1} \\
&\quad \text{vec}(B_\theta B_\theta').
\end{aligned}
$$

Let us now turn to the monthly version of the observation equation. We will start by analyzing the (not very realistic) case in which all variables are observable at monthly frequency. The monthly observation equation would then be:

---

[1] If capacity utilization is instead already stationary in the level, then $x_{j,t_m} = \frac{1}{3}(CU_{t_m} + CU_{t_m-1} + CU_{t_m-2})$, which corresponds to the average capacity utilization over the quarter.

$$Y_{t_m} = M_m(L) s_{t_m}, \qquad (3)$$

where

$$M_m(L) = (M_{0,\theta} + 0 \cdot L + 0 \cdot L^2 + M_{1,\theta} L^3 + \ldots + M_{p,\theta} L^{3p}).$$

The equations (2) and (3) therefore describe the dynamics that are compatible with the quarterly model. If all the observables of the model were available at a monthly frequency, we could now simply use the monthly model defined by equations (2) and (3) to immediately incorporate this higher frequency information. However, some variables – think of GDP, for example – are not available at monthly frequency. So let us assume, that the variable in the i-th position of the vector of observables $Y_{t_m}$, i.e. $y_{i,t_m}$, is not available at a monthly frequency, but only at the quarterly frequency. This means that $y_{i,t_m}$ is a latent variable when $t_m$ does not correspond to the end of a quarter. Moreover, due to the unsynchronized data releases schedule data are not available on the same span (the dataset has jagged edges). The unavailability of some data does not prevent us from still taking advantage of the monthly information that is available using a Kalman filter. To do so, we follow Giannone, Reichlin and Small (2008) and define the following state space model:

$$s_{t_m} = T_m s_{t_m - 1} + B_m \varepsilon_{m,t_m},$$
$$Y_{t_m} = M_m(L) s_{t_m} + V_{t_m},$$

where $V_{t_m} = (v_{1,t_m}, \ldots, v_{k,t_m})$ is such that $var(v_{i,t_m}) = 0$ if $y_{i,t_m}$ is available and $var(v_{i,t_m}) = \infty$ otherwise.

Let us now turn to how we incorporate the auxiliary monthly variables. As a starting point, we define the relation between the auxiliary variables $X_{t_q}$ and the model's observable variables at a quarterly frequency:

$$X_{t_q} = \mu + \Lambda Y_{t_q} + e_{t_q}, \qquad (4)$$

where $e_{t_q}$ is orthogonal to the quarterly variables entering the model. Given that some of the observables are available only at a quarterly frequency, we will use this equation to estimate the coefficients $\Lambda$ and the variance-covariance matrix of the shocks $E(e_{t_q} e_{t_q}') = R$. Let us now focus on incorporating the auxiliary variables in their monthly form. As stressed above, $X_{t_m} = (x_{1,t}, \ldots, x_{n,t})'$ is the vector of these auxiliary stationary monthly variables transformed so as to correspond to quarterly quantities at the end of each quarter. We can relate $X_{t_m}$ to the monthly observables $Y_{t_m}$ using the equivalent of equation (4) for the monthly frequency (the bridge model):

$$X_{t_m} = \mu + \Lambda Y_{t_m} + e_{t_m}, \qquad (5)$$

where $e_{t_m} = (e_{1,t_m}, \ldots, e_{k,t_m})$ is such that $var(e_{i,t_m}) = [R]_{i,i}$ if $X_{i,t_m}$ is available and $var(e_{i,t_m}) = \infty$ otherwise. This way, we take care of the problem of the jagged edge at the end of the dataset, due to the fact that the data is released in an unsynchronized fashion and that the variables have different publishing lags (e.g. Capacity utilization releases refer to the *previous* month's total capacity utilization, while the release of the Philadelphia Business Outlook Survey refers to the *current* month). We will use equation (5) to expand the original state space:

$$s_{t_m} = T_m s_{t_m - 1} + B_m \varepsilon_{m,t_m},$$
$$Y_{t_m} = M_m(L) s_{t_m} + V_{t_m}, \qquad (6)$$
$$X_{t_m} - \mu = \Lambda M_m(L) s_{t_m} + e_{t_m},$$

where $V_{t_m}$ and $e_{t_m}$ are defined above. The state space form (6) allows us to account for and incorporate all the information about the missing observables contained in the auxiliary variables.

The choice of modeling $X_{t_m}$ as solely dependent on the observables, rather than depending in a more general way from the states, is motivated by the fact that we want the auxiliary variables to be relevant *only* when the quarterly data is not available. Indeed, with this modeling approach, the monthly auxiliary information becomes redundant, when the quarterly data is available. This would not have been the case, if we had bridged the monthly variables directly with the states, because in this case we could have exploited the auxiliary variables to get better estimates of the latent state variables, even when the data for the observables became fully available.

Moreover, the choice of modeling the bridge model as a function of the observables only is not model dependent. The estimation of the coefficient $\Lambda$ depends exclusively on the data and the model enters the bridge equation solely by imposing the transitional dynamics. This feature is nice, because it yields more robustness.

In the following section we present an application of the methodology described above.

### Design of the Forecasting Exercise

We use a simple New-Keynesian dynamic stochastic general equilibrium model, as the one used in Del Negro and Schorfheide (2004). The only source of nominal rigidities in this model is the presence of adjustment costs that firms incur in when changing their prices. A detailed description of the model is reported in an appendix available on the authors' website, while here we present only the log-linearized model.

The log-linearized system can be reduced to three equations in output, inflation and the interest rate:

$$\hat{y}_t - \hat{g}_t = E_t(\hat{y}_{t+1} - \hat{g}_{t+1})$$

$$-\frac{1}{\tau}(\hat{r}_t - E_t\hat{\pi}_{t+1} - \rho_z\hat{z}_t),$$

$$\hat{\pi}_t = \beta\, E_t\hat{\pi}_{t+1} + \kappa\,(\hat{y}_t - \hat{g}_t), \qquad (7)$$

$$\hat{r}_t = \psi_1\,(1 - \rho_r)\,\hat{\pi}_t$$

$$+ \psi_2\,(1 - \rho_r)\,\hat{y}_t + \rho_r\hat{r}_{t-1} + \varepsilon_{r,t}.$$

The first equation relates current output gap $(\hat{y}_t - \hat{g}_t$, because we are in presence of government spending) with the expected future output gap, the real interest rate $(\hat{r}_t - E_t\hat{\pi}_{t+1})$ and the shocks to the technology process $\hat{z}_t$, which is assumed to evolve following the process:

$$\hat{z}_{t+1} = \rho_z\,\hat{z}_t + \varepsilon_t^z.$$

Also the government spending shock follows an AR(1) process:

$$\hat{g}_{t+1} = \rho_g\hat{g}_t + \varepsilon_t^g.$$

The second equation is the familiar New-Keynesian Phillips curve and the last equation is a standard Taylor rule.

The relation between log-deviations from steady state and observable output growth, CPI inflation and the annualized nominal interest rate is given by the following measurement equation:

$$\text{INFL}_t = \pi^* + 4\hat{\pi}_t,$$
$$\text{RA}_t = \pi^* + r^* + 4\hat{r}_t, \qquad (8)$$
$$\Delta\ln\text{GDP}_t = \ln\gamma + \hat{y}_t - \hat{y}_{t-1} + \hat{z}_t.$$

The model given by equations (7) can then be solved with standard techniques, such as those proposed by Blanchard and Kahn (1980), Uhlig (1999), Klein (2000), Sims (2002), among others. More specifically, the model has a solution in terms:

$$s_t = \begin{bmatrix} \hat{r}_t \\ \hat{g}_t \\ \hat{z}_t \end{bmatrix} = A_\theta\, s_{t-1} + B_\theta \varepsilon_t, \qquad (9)$$

$$Y_t = \begin{bmatrix} INFL_t \\ RA_t \\ \Delta \ln GDP_t \end{bmatrix} = C_\theta(L)\, s_t.$$

For simplicity, we perform the estimation of the underlying parameters $\theta$ only once at the beginning of the evaluation sample, i.e. in 1997Q1, using data for the period 1982Q1 to 1996Q4.

We want to show how to incorporate a set of monthly variables into the prototypical New-Keynesian model defined above, obtaining forecasts that are more accurate than the ones based solely on the model and, what is more important, real-time estimates of model-based concepts such as TFP growth and the natural rate of interest.

Clearly the model (9) has the form of the state space model (1) and hence it is possible to determine its monthly dynamics as described in the previous section. We perform the forecasting exercise over the evaluation sample 1997Q1-2007Q4 using quarter-on-quarter GDP growth, CPI annualized quarterly inflation, the annualized Fed Funds Rate and a panel of series that are deemed to be informative on the state on the economy, e.g. the ones NBER Business Cycle Dating Committee looks at or the ones that Bloomberg reports. More specifically, the series we use are the following: Purchasing Managers' Index, Total construction put in place, Total employment on non aggregate payrolls, Average hourly earnings, Total industrial production, Total capacity utilization, the Index of general activity of the Philadelphia Fed Business Outlook Survey, Producers price indices for finished goods and crude materials (for both 1982=100), Total sales, Total inventories, Real disposable personal income, and Total personal consumption expenditures.

*Table 2* describes a stylized calendar of data releases where variables have been grouped in twenty-three clusters according to their timeliness. The stylization consists in associating a date with a group of variables with similar economic content (soft, quantities, prices and so

*Table 1*

**Prior and Posterior Distribution of the Parameters of the Model Estimated over the Period 1982Q1 to 1996Q4**

| | PRIOR DISTRIBUTION | | | POSTERIOR DISTRIBUTION | | |
| | Distribution | Mean | Std dev | Mode | Mean | Std dev |
|---|---|---|---|---|---|---|
| $\gamma$ | Normal | 0.5 | 0.5 | 0.6815 | 0.6924 | 0.1251 |
| $\pi^*$ | Gamma | 5 | 2 | 3.8862 | 4.3852 | 1.3813 |
| $r^*$ | Gamma | 2 | 1 | 3.0139 | 3.0022 | 0.5148 |
| $\tau$ | Gamma | 2 | 0.5 | 2.8826 | 2.9628 | 0.5015 |
| $\kappa$ | Gamma | 0.3 | 0.1 | 0.1188 | 0.1528 | 0.0500 |
| $\psi_1$ | Gamma | 1.5 | 0.5 | 1.0369 | 1.5420 | 0.3651 |
| $\psi_2$ | Gamma | 0.125 | 0.1 | 0.0951 | 0.2719 | 0.0320 |
| $\rho_g$ | Beta | 0.9 | 0.05 | 0.9656 | 0.9648 | 0.0200 |
| $\rho_z$ | Beta | 0.2 | 0.1 | 0.3244 | 0.3265 | 0.1107 |
| $\rho_r$ | Beta | 0.7 | 0.15 | 0.8048 | 0.8279 | 0.0359 |
| $\sigma_g$ | InvGamma | 1.25 | 0.65 | 0.4924 | 0.5066 | 0.0706 |
| $\sigma_z$ | InvGamma | 1.25 | 0.65 | 0.5927 | 0.6404 | 0.0754 |
| $\sigma_r$ | InvGamma | 0.63 | 0.33 | 0.7155 | 0.7310 | 0.0794 |

on). This is a quite realistic representation of the calendar and will allow us to evaluate the changes in the forecast due to the release of new data on variables with different economic content. In the first column of *Table 2* we indicate the approximate date of the release, in the second the series and in the third the publication lag. We can see, for example, that the Philadelphia Fed Survey is the first release referring to the current month m and it is published the last day of the first month of the quarter. Hard data arrive later. For example, industrial production is published in the middle of the second month of the quarter and refers to the previous month. GDP, released the last week of the last month of the quarter refers to the previous quarter.

The forecast will be updated twenty-three times throughout the quarter, corresponding to the stylized calendar 2. In this way we can associate to each update a date and a set of variables. The horizontal axis of the Figures below, reporting the results, indicate the grouping of releases corresponding to the calendar.

## Empirical Results

### Forecast Accuracy

*Figure 1*, shows how the mean square forecast errors (MSFE) of the nowcasts of GDP growth produced with the quarterly DSGE model (Q) and with the monthly DSGE model that also exploits the information contained in the panel (M+panel) change with the arrival of new information within the quarter. Also a naive benchmark is shown for comparison.[2] In the case of GDP growth the naive benchmark is a constant growth model (random walk in levels) which is estimated as the mean of the last 10 years GDP growths. Notice that it changes in correspondence with panel 7, that is when we can incorporate the data of GDP growth in

the last quarter, which was not available in the previous 5 panels.

We also compare the performance of Q and M+panel with the performance of the SPF's nowcast of GDP growth. Since the SPF forecasts are released approximately around the middle of the second month of the quarter, we choose to match it with forecasts produced with approximately the same information, i.e. in the second month of the quarter, between the employment release and the Philadelphia Fed Business Outlook Survey release.

As mentioned above, the parameters of the DSGE model are estimated once, at the beginning of the evaluation sample, and are kept fix hence forth. The coefficients that load the observables of the DSGE into the rest of the panel are instead re-estimated at every step.

Results show that, in the first month, the information flow has very little impact on the MSFE of GDP nowcasts made with the monthly model that exploits the panel. This is because during the first month, until the arrival of the data for that month's Fed Funds Rate at the very end of the month, all the information being released involves the previous quarter. As soon as information on the current quarter starts to arrive (with the Fed Funds Rate, PMI and the employment situation of the first month of the quarter, which all arrive at the beginning of the second month), we start seeing the positive impact of the new information on the accuracy of the predictions. Moreover, comparing the nowcast of GDP produced with the monthly model that exploits the information available at the middle of the second month with the SPF nowcasts, one can see that the M+panel model does as good as, if not better, than the SPF. The smooth decline in the MSFE of GDP nowcasts of the monthly model implies that each of the new releases carries some information that is

---

[2] We chose to present the results in absolute rather than in relative terms, in order to better highlight the arrival of the information and the impact it has on the various models, including the benchmark.

Table 2

**Data Releases are Indicated in Rows. Column 1 Indicates the Official Dates of the Publication. Column 2 Indicates the Releases. Column 3 Indicates the Publishing Lag: E.g. IP is Released with 1-month delay (m-1)**

| | TIMING | RELEASE | PUBLICATION LAG |
|---|---|---|---|
| 1 | 1st day of the 1st month of the quarter | – | – |
| 2 | 1st business day of the 1st month of the quarter | PMI and construction | m-1 |
| 3 | 1st Friday of the 1st month of the quarter | Employment situation | m-1 |
| 4 | 15th to 17th of the 1st month of the quarter | Industrial Production and Capacity Utilization | m-1 |
| 5 | 3rd Thursday of the 1st month of the quarter | Business Outlook Survey: Philadelphia Fed | m |
| 6 | Middle of the 1st month of the quarter | CPI and PPI | m-1 |
| 7 | Last week of the 1st month of the quarter | GDP release | q-1 |
| 8 | Day after GDP release | Inventories, Sales, PCE, RDPI | m-2 (INV and sales), m-1 (PCE,RDPI) |
| 9 | Last day of the 1st month of the quarter | Fed Funds Rate | m |
| 10 | 1st business day of the 2nd month of the quarter | PMI and construction | m-1 |
| 11 | 1st Friday of the 2nd month of the quarter | Employment situation | m-1 |
| 12 | 15th to 17th of the 2nd month of the quarter | Industrial Production and Capacity Utilization | m-1 |
| 13 | 3rd Thursday of the 2nd month of the quarter | Business Outlook Survey: Philadelphia Fed | m |
| 14 | Middle of the 2nd month of the quarter | CPI and PPI | m-1 |
| 15 | Last week of the 2nd month of the quarter | Inventories, Sales, PCE, RDPI | m-2 (INV and sales), m-1 (PCE, RDPI) |
| 16 | Last day of the 2nd month of the quarter | Fed Funds Rate | m |
| 17 | 1st business day of the 3rd month of the quarter | PMI and construction | m-1 |
| 18 | 1st Friday of the 3rd month of the quarter | Employment situation | m-1 |
| 19 | 15th to 17th of the 3rd month of the quarter | Industrial Production and Capacity Utilization | m-1 |
| 20 | 3rd Thursday of the 3rd month of the quarter | Business Outlook Survey: Philadelphia Fed | m-1 |
| 21 | Middle of the 3rd month of the quarter | CPI and PPI | m-1 |
| 22 | Last week of the 3rd month of the quarter | Inventories, Sales, PCE, RDPI | m-2 (INV and sales),m-1(PCE,RDPI) |
| 23 | Last day of the 3rd month of the quarter | Fed Funds Rate | m |

relevant for predicting today's GDP growth accurately.

*Figures 2* and *3* report the mean square forecast errors (MSFE) of the nowcasts for CPI year-on-year inflation and the annualized Fed Funds Rate, respectively, produced with the quarterly DSGE model (Q) and with the monthly DSGE model that also exploits the information contained in the panel (M+panel), and compares them to a naive benchmark (NB). We construct nowcasts of CPI year-on-year inflation as the mean of the last three available data points for annualized quarterly CPI inflation and the nowcast of annualized quarterly CPI inflation produced with each of the models we compare. Similarly, the one-step-ahead forecast of CPI year-on-year inflation is the mean of the last two

available data points for annualized quarterly CPI inflation and the nowcast and one-step-ahead forecasts of (annualized) quarterly GDP generated by the models under consideration. The naive model for CPI year-on-year inflation is the last available year-on-year inflation: It is constructed, using quarterly data, as the mean of the last 4 available data points. This means that, as is obvious from *Figure 3*, the benchmark will change when the data for CPI inflation of the last quarter becomes available, i.e. at panel 6. The naive model for the Fed Funds Rate is a random walk, that is we assume that the Fed Funds Rate today is equal to the Fed Funds Rate of the previous quarter. Hence, when the information on the Fed Funds Rate for this quarter becomes available, i.e. in panel 23, the errors go to zero.

## Figure 1

**NOWCAST GDP Growth:**

**MSFE Across Vintages Throughout the Month**

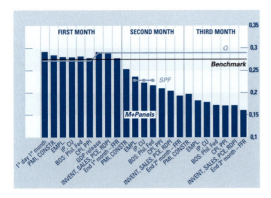

## Figure 2

**NOWCAST CPI Inflation:**

**MSFE Across Vintages Throughout the Month**

## Figure 3

**NOWCAST Fed Funds Rate:**

**MSFE Across Vintages Throughout the Month**

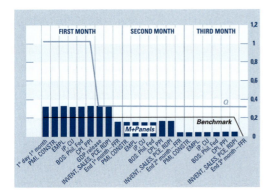

As for GDP growth, also the accuracy of the predictions of CPI year-on-year inflation and the Fed Funds Rate improves as more information is released. However, the step shape of *Figure 2 and Figure 3* indicates that the variables of the panel are not very relevant in improving the accuracy of the forecasts of CPI inflation and the Fed Funds Rate, respectively; it is just the arrival of more data points of the forecasted variables that helps.

*Tables 3-5* report the MSFE of nowcasts and forecasts up to 4 quarters ahead, for GDP growth, year-on-year CPI inflation and the Fed Funds Rate, respectively. We compare the naive model, the quarterly DSGE model (Q), the monthly DSGE model (M) and the monthly DSGE model that also exploits the information contained in the panel (M+panel) with the forecasts produced by SPF. Hence, in order to match the information available to them at the time of the forecast, we generate the forecasts of *Tables 3-5* with "panel 12", i.e. corresponding to the release of Industrial Production and Capacity utilization data in the second month of each quarter.

Looking at *Tables 3-5*, two results are worth mentioning. First, the performance of the M model (i.e. the monthly model that does not exploit the panel) when nowcasting, is quite close to the performance of the quarterly model. This implies, that the improvement obtained with the M+panel model really derives from the extra-information and not from the monthly dynamics. Second, notice how, as the forecasting horizon increases, the performance of the Q, M and M+panel models becomes more and more similar. That is, the information that can be extracted for the panel of variables is relevant only when nowcasting.

*Figures 4-6* depict, respectively for GDP growth, year-on year CPI inflation and the Fed Funds Rate, the nowcasts produced by the

Table 3

**Mean Square Forecast Errors of Quarter-on-Quarter GDP Growth Forecasts with Horizons 0 to 4 for the Different Model Relative to the Naive Benchmark**

| | NB | SPF | Q | M | M+panel |
|---|---|---|---|---|---|
| **Q0** | 0.275 | 0.226 | 0.289 | 0.275 | 0.223 |
| **Q1** | 0.281 | 0.272 | 0.278 | 0.281 | 0.278 |
| **Q2** | 0.274 | 0.287 | 0.269 | 0.272 | 0.270 |
| **Q3** | 0.269 | 0.272 | 0.261 | 0.263 | 0.262 |
| **Q4** | 0.276 | 0.280 | 0.264 | 0.266 | 0.265 |

Table 4

**Mean Square Forecast Errors of CPI Year-on-Year Inflation Forecasts with Horizons 0 to 4 for the Different Model Relative to the Naive Benchmark**

| | NB | SPF | Q | M | M+panel |
|---|---|---|---|---|---|
| **Q0** | 0.058 | 0.059 | 0.123 | 0.123 | 0.114 |
| **Q1** | 0.196 | 0.181 | 0.440 | 0.440 | 0.423 |
| **Q2** | 0.306 | 0.367 | 0.494 | 0.519 | 0.473 |
| **Q3** | 0.447 | 0.572 | 0.713 | 0.740 | 0.672 |
| **Q4** | 0.594 | 0.713 | 1.092 | 1.132 | 1.059 |

Table 5

**Mean Square Forecast Errors of Forecasts for the Fed Funds Rate with Horizons 0 to 4 for the Different Model Relative to the Naive Benchmark**

| | NB | Q | M | M+panel |
|---|---|---|---|---|
| **Q0** | 0.2036 | 0.3306 | 0.1586 | 0.1530 |
| **Q1** | 0.7291 | 1.0436 | 0.7705 | 0.7440 |
| **Q2** | 1.5083 | 1.8856 | 1.5822 | 1.5285 |
| **Q3** | 2.4527 | 2.7757 | 2.4775 | 2.4025 |
| **Q4** | 3.4712 | 3.6764 | 3.3953 | 3.3136 |

naive model, the Q model and M+panel model, at different dates in the quarter, and hence with different information available to forecast.[3] The top-left panel of each graph report the nowcasts generated with panel 6, i.e. in the first month of the quarter, right after the release of the data for prices. The top-right panel graphs the nowcasts produced with "panel 12", the day of the release of Industrial Production and Capacity utilization data in the second month of each quarter. Since the information, in this case, approximately matches the one available to the SPF when they produce their forecasts, we include the latter in the graph. The bottom-left panel of *Figures 4-6* plots the nowcasts generated by the various models the day of the release of employment data in the third month of the quarter (panel 18). Finally, the bottom-right panel reports the nowcasts produced at the end of the third month of each quarter, once the information on that quarter's Fed Funds Rate becomes available.

It is evident from *Figure 4* that the nowcast produced in real-time with the M+panel model is effective at tracking GDP growth and that it compares well with the SPF. Moreover, a general look to both *Figures 1-3* and *Figures 4-6* allows us to make the following conclusions. First, while the performance of the M+panel model in forecasting GDP is exceptional, the M+panel model is not as effective in estimating CPI inflation, where the benchmark beats all models. Its performance with respect to the Fed funds is instead quite good. *Figures 1-3* highlight the marginal impacts of data releases on the accuracy of the nowcasts of the variables of interest. While the smooth decline in the MSFE of the GDP nowcasts indicates that, from the second month on, all new releases improve the accuracy of the forecast, the step-shape of *Figures 2* and *3* implies that the only relevant information for these two variables are their own releases.

---

[3] The different information sets are identified with the progressive number of *Table 2*. So, for example, panel 12 is the panel obtained as a snapshot of the information available right after the release, in the second month of the quarter, of the IP and CU for the first month of the quarter.

## Structural Analysis

The second set of results involves the structural features of the models. Given that we have a fully-fledged structural model, we can use it to forecast and analyze quantities that are unobserved and intrinsically meaningful only within the context of a structural model, such as the TFP.

Since the variable "TFP" is unobserved, we take its ex-post estimate – i.e. the estimate produced by the quarterly DSGE model using all available data up to 2007Q4 – to be the "true" one. Then we try to match, in real-time, this ex-post estimate of the TFP using the Q model (the quarterly model that uses only the "quarterly" observable variables) and the M+panel model (the monthly model that exploits the variables of the panel). We also construct a series of "TFP" estimates intrinsic

in the SPF forecasts; we obtain these by taking the SPF nowcasts and forecasts for GDP and CPI year-on-year inflation as if they were "actual" data and that feeds into the quarterly DSGE (Q) model. The filter will return a series for the TFP which now accounts for the SPF nowcasts and forecasts.

*Figure 7* shows how the mean square forecast errors (MSFE) of the nowcasts of TFP growth produced with the quarterly DSGE model (Q) and with the monthly DSGE model that also exploits the information contained in the panel (M+panel) change with the arrival of new information within the quarter. We report also the MSFE of a naive benchmark, a constant growth model (random walk in levels) which is estimated as the mean of the last 10 years' TFP growths. We also compare the performance of Q and M+panel with the performance of

*Figure 4*

**NOWCAST of GDP for 4 Representative Vintages**

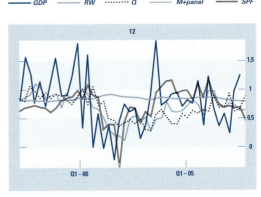

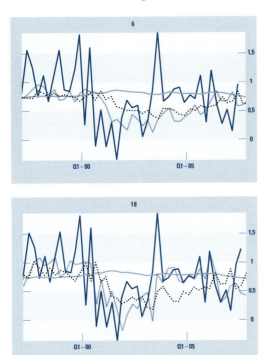

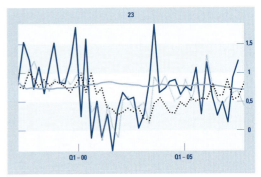

the SPF's nowcast of TFP growth, obtained as specified above.

*Figure 8* depicts the nowcasts of TFP growth produced with by the naive model, the Q model and M+panel model, at different dates in the quarter, and hence with different information available to forecast. The top-left panel of each graph report the nowcasts generated with panel 6, i.e. in the first month of the quarter, right after the release of the data for prices. The top-right panel graphs the nowcasts produced with "panel 12", the day of the release of Industrial Production and Capacity utilization data in the second month of each quarter. Since the information, in this case, approximately matches the one available to the SPF when they produce their forecasts, we include the latter in the graph. The bottom-left panel of *Figure 8* plots the nowcasts generated by the various

models the day of the release of employment data in the third month of the quarter. Finally, the bottom-right panel reports the nowcasts produced at the end of the third month of each quarter, once the information on that quarter's Fed Funds Rate becomes available.

*Table 6* reports the MSFE for nowcasts and forecasts up to 4 quarters ahead of TFP growth. We compare the naive benchmark of a constant growth model, the quarterly DSGE model (Q), the monthly DSGE model (M) and the monthly DSGE model that also exploits the information contained in the panel (M+panel) with the forecasts produced by SPF.

Hence, in order to match the information available to them at the time of the forecast, we generate the forecasts of *Tables 3-5* with "panel 12", i.e. corresponding to the release of

*Figure 5*

**NOWCAST of CPI for 4 Representative Vintages**

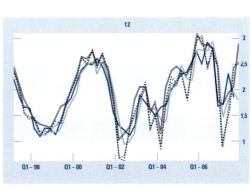

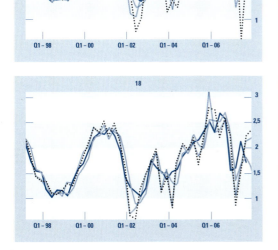

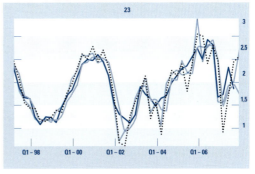

*Figure 6*

**NOWCAST of RA for 4 Representative Vintages**

—— int.rate  —— RW  —— M+panel  ········ Q  —— SPF

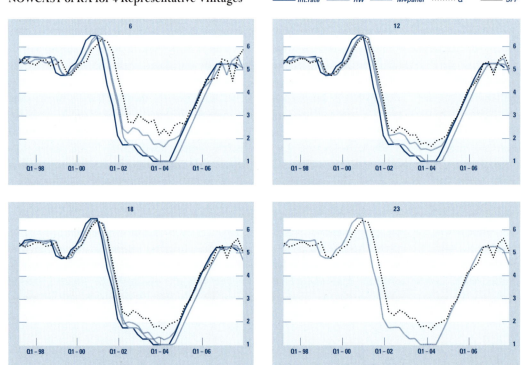

*Figure 7*

**NOWCAST TFP Growth: MSFE Across Vintages Throughout the Month**

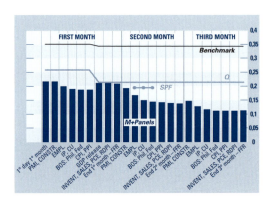

*Table 6*

**Mean Square Forecast Errors of TFP Growth Forecasts with Horizons 0 to 4 for the Different Model Relative to the Naive Benchmark**

|    | NB | SPF | Q | M+panel |
|----|------|------|------|------|
| Q0 | 0.3437 | 0.1925 | 0.2128 | 0.1505 |
| Q1 | 0.3639 | 0.302 | 0.2647 | 0.2425 |
| Q2 | 0.3639 | 0.338 | 0.2839 | 0.2761 |
| Q3 | 0.3686 | 0.343 | 0.2862 | 0.2846 |
| Q4 | 0.3844 | 0.346 | 0.2951 | 0.2942 |

Industrial Production and Capacity utilization data in the second month of each quarter.

The set of tables and graphs we present for TFP allow us to draw the following conclusions. First, the information extracted from the panel can only be exploited effectively when estimating current TFP growth. However, this information is very useful in the current quarter and allows to track very well the ex-post estimate of TFP, the better, the more advanced we are in the quarter. A part from the improvement in accuracy of the forecasts of the estimates, which was clear also from the previous subsection, the highlight of this exercise is that we are able to track – quite well and in real-time – an important unobservable quantity of the DSGE model. Hence, the model becomes a tool to interpret reality also within the quarter. In this sense, we have bridged conjunctural analysis with structural models.

## Conclusions

This chapter proposes a formal method to link the real time flow of information within the quarter to quarterly structural DSGE models. We show how to define the monthly dynamics compatible with the DSGE model and how to expand its state space representation to incorporate information from monthly variables which are used in conjunctural analysis to derive early estimates. Our procedure allows to produce early estimates of key observable quantities considered in the model, before they become available. It can also be used to obtain early estimates of unobserved key variables such as total factor productivity or the natural interest rate. A by-product of this methodology is the possibility of computing the response of the non-modeled variables to the structural shocks in the DSGE model, as we show in Giannone, Monti and Reichlin (2008).

*Figure 8*

**Real-Time Estimate of TFP Growth**

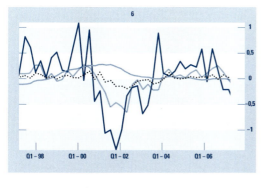

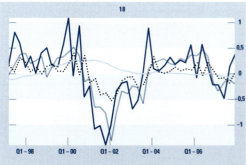

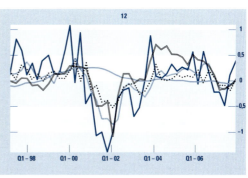

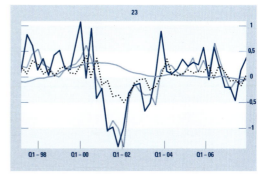

The approach presented in this chapter has two limitations, which are however addressed in Giannone, Monti and Reichlin (2008). First, in the simple prototypical DSGE model we use knowing the history of the observables is sufficient to extract the states, i.e. the model is fundamental. For more complex models, e.g. models that have more states than observables, this might not be the case, and it might thus be important to link the variables directly with the states. Second, here we are assuming that the idiosyncratic components are i.i.d. and cross-sectionally orthogonal. We know that estimates are quite robust to this assumption but by modeling the dynamics and cross-correlations directly we can improve the quality and the understanding of the model. Both these issues can be addressed by estimating a large VAR, as in Banbura et al. (2008), in which we impose the dynamics of the DSGE model on the transition of the states and estimate the remaining dynamic relations.

The empirical application is based on a prototypical three equations DSGE model à la Del Negro and Schorfheide (2004) which we augment with thirteen monthly variables. We show how the model-compatible estimates of GDP, inflation, the Federal Funds Rate and total factor productivity evolve throughout the quarter and become more accurate as increasingly more information becomes available.

# REFERENCES

**Aastveit, K. A., and T. G. Trovik.** 2008. "Nowcasting Norwegian GDP: The role of asset prices in a small open economy." Norges Bank Working Paper 2007/09.

**Adolfson, M., S. Laséen, J. Lindé, and L. E. O. Svensson.** 2008. "Optimal Monetary Policy in an Operational Medium-Sized DSGE Model." National Bureau of Economic Research Working Paper 14092.

**Anderson, B. D. O., and J. B. Moore.** 1979. *Optimal Filtering.* Prentice-Hall.

**Anderson, E., L. P. Hansen, E. R. McGrattan, and T. J. Sargent.** 1996. "Mechanics of Forming and Estimating Dynamic Linear Economies." In *Handbook of Computational Economics*, Volume 1, ed. D. A. K. Hans, M. Amman, and J. Rust, 171–252. North-Holland.

**Angelini, E., G. Camba-Méndez, D. Giannone, G. Rünstler, and L. Reichlin.** 2008. "Short-term forecasts of euro area GDP growth." ECB mimeo.

**Banbura, M., D. Giannone, and L. Reichlin.** 2008. "Large Bayesian VARs." European Central Bank Working Paper Series 966.

**Blanchard, O. J., and C. M. Kahn.** 1980. "The Solution of Linear Difference Models under Rational Expectations." *Econometrica*, 48(5): 1305-1311.

**Boivin, J., and M. Giannoni.** 2006. "DSGE Models in a Data-Rich Environment." National Bureau of Economic Research Working Paper 12772.

**Christiano, L. J., M. Eichenbaum, and C. L. Evans.** 2005. "Nominal Rigidities and the Dynamic Effects of a Shock to Monetary Policy." *Journal of Political Economy*, 113 (1): 1–45.

**Christoffel, K., G. Coenen, and A. Warne.** 2008. "The new area-wide model of the euro area – a micro-founded open-economy model for forecasting and policy analysis." European Central Bank Working Paper Series 944.

**Del Negro, M., and F. Schorfheide.** 2004. "Priors from General Equilibrium Models for VARs." *International Economic Review*, 45: 643–673.

**Del Negro, M., F. Schorfheide, F. Smets, and R. Wouters.** 2007. „On the Fit of New Keynesian Models." *Journal of Business and Economic Statistics*, 25: 123-143.

**Forni, M., M. Hallin, M. Lippi, and L. Reichlin.** 2000. "The Generalized Dynamic Factor Model: Identification and Estimation." *Review of Economics and Statistics*, 82(4): 540-554.

**Giacomini, R., and H. White.** 2006. "Tests of Conditional Predictive Ability." *Econometrica*, 74(6): 1545-1578.

**Giannone, D., L. Reichlin, and D. Small.** 2008. "Nowcasting GDP and Inflation: The Real Time Informational Content of Macroeconomic Data Releases." *Journal of Monetary Economics*, 55(4): 665-676.

**Giannone, D., F. Monti, and L. Reichlin.** 2008. "Short-term Analysis with Structural Models." London Business School Mimeo.

**Klein, P.** 2000. "Using the Generalized Schur Form to Solve a System of Linear Expectational Difference Equations." *Journal of Economic Dynamics and Control*, 24(10): 1405-1423.

**Matheson, T.** 2007. "An analysis of the informational content of New Zealand data releases: The importance of business opinion surveys." Reserve Bank of New Zealand Discussion Paper Series DP2007/13, revised.

**Rotemberg, J., and M. Woodford.** 1997. "An optimization-based econometric framework for the evaluation of monetary policy." In *NBER macroeconomics annual 1997*, ed. B. S. Bernanke and J. J. Rotemberg, 297-346.

**Smets, F., and R. Wouters.** 2003. "An Estimated Dynamic Stochastic General Equilibrium Model of the Euro Area." *Journal of the European Economic Association*, 1 (5): 1123–175.

**Sims, C. A.** 2002. "Solving Linear Rational Expectations Models." *Computational Economics*, 20(1-2): 1-20.

# MONEY IN MONETARY POLICY DESIGN: MONETARY CROSS-CHECKING IN THE NEW-KEYNESIAN MODEL*

**Guenter W. Beck (Goethe University Frankfurt and CFS)**
**Volker Wieland (Goethe University Frankfurt, CEPR and CFS)**

## Introduction

The notion that inflation is a monetary phenomenon is a central tenet of monetary economics. It implies that inflation is ultimately a consequence of monetary policy, and the same conclusion is applied to deflation. This view is usually motivated by the quantity theory. The quantity theory states that sustained increases or decreases in the overall price level occur along with faster or slower growth rates of monetary aggregates adjusted for long-run output and velocity trends. On the basis of this theory, central banks have at times assigned an important role to monetary aggregates in the formulation of monetary policy. For example, the U.S. Federal Reserve emphasized the role of monetary aggregates when Chairman Paul Volcker set out to overcome the great inflation in the United States in 1979. Perhaps, he was partly following the earlier example of the German Bundesbank that had been more successful in fighting the inflationary impetus of the 1970s oil price shocks with the help of monetary targets.

Recent monetary theory, however, has questioned the usefulness of monetary aggregates for monetary policy. For example, Woodford (2006) asks "How important is money in the conduct of monetary policy?"[1] and responds:

*"I believe that a serious examination of the reasons given thus far for assigning a prominent role to monetary aggregates in (policy) deliberations provides little support for a continued emphasis on those aggregates."*

With regard to further efforts aimed at achieving a better understanding of the

---

* An earlier version of this paper was presented at the Deutsche Bank Prize Symposium 2007 on "The Theory and Practice of Monetary Policy Today" in honor of the prize winner Professor Michael Woodford from Columbia University. We are grateful for comments on this research by participants at the conference, and in particular by Michael Woodford, Stefan Gerlach, Robert Lucas, Mathias Hoffmann, Jagjit Chadha, Alex Cukierman, John B. Taylor and Ignazio Angeloni. The usual disclaimer applies.

[1] This question formed the title of his contribution to the Fourth ECB Central Banking Conference "The Role of Money: Money and Monetary Policy in the Twenty-First Century", November 9-10, 2006.

dynamics of monetary aggregates Michael Woodford concludes:

*"... There is at present little reason ... to devote much attention to questions such as the construction of improved measures of the money supply or improved econometric models of money demand. For there is little intelligible connection between those questions and the kinds of uncertainty about the effects of monetary policy that are the actual obstacles to the development of more effective, more reliable and more transparent ways of conducting policy."*

These conclusions are based on the New-Keynesian model of monetary policy. This model as laid out by Rotemberg and Woodford (1997) and Goodfriend and King (1997) and developed in detail in Woodford (2003) has quickly become the principal workhorse model in monetary economics. Requiring only a small number of equations and variables the model has proved very useful in deriving several important principles for the conduct of monetary policy (see for example, Kerr and King (1996) and Clarida et al. (1999)). It suggests that optimal interest rate policy ought to be conducted with reference to inflation forecasts and output gaps but without direct concern for monetary aggregates.

The importance of monetary aggregates has also declined in central bank practice. For example, the U.S. Fed already de-emphasized the role of monetary aggregates in its strategy in the early 1990s, but perhaps more because of empirical difficulties than because of new theories. Also, nowadays no central bank pursues a strategy of monetary targeting. The Bundesbank's difficulties with meeting short-term monetary growth targets also became very apparent in the 1990s.

Nevertheless, some central banks and some monetary theorists still hold out for a special role for money in the formulation of monetary policy. The European Central Bank did not adopt the Bundesbank's monetary targets but it maintains that its monetary analysis is important enough to deserve particular consideration separately from its other economic analysis. Otmar Issing, the ECB's former chief economist, describes the separate monetary pillar in the ECB strategy as follows:

*"In line with the argument of a closer relationship between money and inflation at lower frequencies, the function ascribed to the monetary pillar is to reveal medium-term risks to price stability .."* but *"... there is no mechanical monetary policy reaction to deviations of M3 growth from the reference value"* and *"... cross-checking the information from the economic analysis with the information from the monetary pillar is ... a crucial element underpinning the robustness and medium-term policy orientation."*

In a recent contribution Lucas (2007) comments on the conflict between the ECB's strategy and the findings of New-Keynesian monetary theory with the following words:

*"Events since 1999 have not tested the importance of the (ECB's) second, monetary pillar, ... I am concerned that this encouraging but brief period of success will foster the opinion, already widely held, that the monetary pillar is superfluous, and lead monetary policy analysis back to the kind of muddled eclecticism that brought us the 1970s inflation."*

Robert Lucas identifies New-Keynesian-style research as one of the possible culprits stating:

*"One source of this concern is the increasing reliance of central bank research on New-Keynesian modeling. New-Keynesian models define monetary policy in terms of a choice of money market rate and so make direct contact with central banking practice. Money supply measures play no role in the estimation, testing or policy simulation of these models. A role for money in the long-run is sometimes verbally acknowledged, but the models themselves are formulated in terms of deviations from trends that are themselves determined somewhere off stage."*

He then goes on to propose the following strategies for research and policy making:

*"It seems likely that these models could be reformulated to give a unified account of trends, including trends in monetary aggregates, and deviations about trend but so far they have not been. This remains an unresolved issue on the frontier of macroeconomic theory. Until it is resolved, monetary information should continue be used as a kind of add-on or cross-check, just as it is in the ECB policy formulation today."*

In this chapter we review the implications of the New-Keynesian model for the role of monetary aggregates and aim to address the criticisms raised by Lucas (2007). We elaborate on earlier work in Beck and Wieland (2008) with a more thorough and detailed exposition of our analysis in the New-Keynesian model. First, we reiterate the case for monetary policy without money. We note that it also applies under conditions of uncertainty as long as certain standard assumptions on the distributions of unobservable variables and error terms are satisfied. Then, we introduce persistent central bank misperceptions regarding unobservables such as potential output or equilibrium interest rates. Such misperceptions lead to persistent policy errors and sustained trends in money growth and inflation. In this manner, we are able to provide a unified account of trends in inflation and monetary aggregates as requested by Lucas (2007).

Beck and Wieland (2007a,b) proposed an interest rate rule that captures the idea of an add-on or cross-check with monetary information in a formal manner.[2] Here, we discuss in detail how to derive the appropriate magnitude of the interest rate adjustment following a significant cross-check with monetary information in the New-Keynesian model. This cross-check is shown to be effective in offsetting persistent deviations of inflation in response to central bank misperceptions.

---

## Optimal Monetary Policy Without Money

In the New-Keynesian model monetary aggregates play no direct role in the transmission of monetary policy to output and inflation. Monetary policy decisions are made with regard to the nominal interest rate. A change in the nominal rate affects the real interest rate because not all prices adjust flexibly and immediately. The presence of such price rigidities introduces real effects of monetary policy. The real interest rate influences aggregate demand. Thus, a change in the real rate can increase or diminish the gap between actual output and the economy's potential that would be realized if the price level would be adjusting flexibly. Changes in the output gap in turn impact on inflation via the New-Keynesian Phillips curve.

Of course, the supply of money is influenced by the open-market operations that the central bank conducts in order to achieve the intended rate of interest. Actual money growth then results from the interplay of money supply and money demand in a recursive manner. The central bank supplies sufficient money to satisfy demand for real balances at the intended rate of interest, the current price level and current income. Consequently, the optimal interest rate policy may be characterized without any recourse to monetary aggregates. From this perspective, efforts to construct better measures of the money supply or to obtain better empirical estimates of the parameters governing money demand are not likely to help improve the performance of monetary policy.

In the following, we present this implication of the New-Keynesian analysis of monetary

---

[2] Our characterization of monetary cross-checking differs from Christiano and Rostagno (2001) who propose an escape clause for Taylor rules that helps exclude the possibility of multiple equilibria and self-fulfilling expectations. This escape clause involves a commitment to monetary targeting if money growth gets of bounds. If effective, it never needs to be implemented.

policy in the context of a simple linearized version of the benchmark model of Rotemberg and Woodford (1997) and Goodfriend and King (1997). This model has been used to study a variety of implications for monetary policy design. A widely-cited example is Clarida et al. (1999). For a detailed exposition of the model and a derivation of the linear approximation the reader is referred to the influential monograph of Woodford (2003).

*The model*

In its simplest form the model consists of two key equations, a forward-looking Phillips curve derived from the firms' pricing problem under monopolistic competition and Calvo-style price rigidity, and an aggregate demand relation, the forward-looking IS curve, that is derived from the households' intertemporal Euler equation. As in Clarida et al. (1999) a money-demand relation may be added as a third behavioral equation in the model.

The linearized Phillips curve relation determines the deviation of inflation, denoted by $\pi_t$, from its steady state, $\bar{\pi}$, as a function of expected future inflation, the output gap and cost-push shocks:

$$\pi_t - \bar{\pi} = \lambda \left( y_t - z_t \right) + \beta \left( \pi_{t+1|t}^e - \bar{\pi} \right) + u_t,$$
$$\text{where } \pi_{t+1|t}^e = E_t \left[ \pi_{t+1} \right]. \tag{1}$$

Expectations regarding future inflation are formed in a rational, forward-looking manner. The output gap is measured as the difference between actual output, $y_t$, and the level of output that would be realized if prices were completely flexible, $z_t$. In the New-Keynesian world this is the appropriate measure of potential or natural output to appear in the Phillips curve relation. The parameter $\lambda$ is a decreasing function of the discount factor $\beta$ and the share of firms that do not adjust their prices in any given period.[3] The

third determinant of inflation in the model, the cost-push shock, is denoted by $u_t$.

The linearized version of the New-Keynesian IS curve then relates actual output, $y_t$, defined as percentage deviation from steady state, to expected future output, the expected real interest rate and a demand shock:

$$y_t = y_{t+1|t}^e - \varphi \left( i_t - \pi_{t+1|t}^e \right) + g_t. \tag{2}$$

The real interest rate is defined as the difference between the short-term nominal interest rate, $i_t$, that is under the control of the central bank and expected inflation. The demand or preference shock is denoted by $g_t$. Clarida et al. (1999) assume that the cost-push and demand shocks are observable at time t and follow AR(1) processes, i.e.:

$$u_t = \rho_u u_{t-1} + \eta_t^u, \tag{3}$$

$$g_t = \rho_g g_{t-1} + \eta_t^g, \tag{4}$$

with $0 \leq \rho_u$, $\rho_g < 1$ and ($\eta_t^g$, $\eta_t^u$) representing mean-zero, i.i.d. disturbances. The unrealistic observability assumption will be abandoned further on in this chapter.

We also follow Clarida et al. (1999) in modeling money demand. Demand for real balances is influenced by the demand for transactions as measured by aggregate income, the opportunity cost as measured by the nominal money market rate and other factors captured by shocks. The respective money demand equation is given by:

$$m_t - p_t = \gamma_y y_t - \gamma_i i_t + s_t. \tag{5}$$

Here, $m_t$ refers to the logarithm of nominal money balances and $p_t$ to the (log of) the price level. Thus, $\Delta p_t = \pi_t$. $\gamma_y$ denotes the

---

[3] More precisely, the parameter $\lambda$ is given by the following expression: $\lambda = (1-\theta)(1-\beta\theta)(\theta)^{-1}$; where $\theta$ denotes the proportion of firms that are not allowed to adjust their prices in a given period.

income elasticity and $\gamma_i$ the semi-interest rate elasticity of money demand. Money demand shocks, $s_t$, are normally distributed with mean zero and variance $\sigma_s^2$. It is possible to derive this specification of money demand from first principles. As shown in Woodford (2003) it requires that utility is separable in consumption and real money balances. Theoretical foundations for a direct role of real money balances in the IS and Phillips curves can be obtained when household utility is not separable in money and consumption. Empirical studies, however, have failed to detect strong direct effects (cf. Ireland (2004) and Andres et al. (2006)) of real balances. Thus, we will exclude this possibility in the remainder of the chapter, while exploring other roles for money in monetary policy design.

*Optimal interest rate policy*

The optimal interest rate policy is determined from the perspective of the central bank's chosen objective. For simplicity, we focus on the objective of a central bank that strictly concentrates on stabilizing actual inflation, $\pi_t$, close to its target denoted by $\pi^*$,

$$\max -\frac{1}{2} E_t \left\{ \sum_{i=0}^{\infty} \beta^i [(\pi_{t+1} - \pi^*)^2] \right\}, \quad (6)$$

subject to the Phillips curve and the IS curve defined by equations (1) and (2). The inflation target is normalized at zero, $\pi^* = 0$. The term "strict inflation targeting" used to describe this strategy was coined by Svensson (1997). It implies that the central bank focuses exclusively on stabilizing inflation without assigning any weight to economic activity in the policy objective.

The associated first-order condition is:

$$E[\pi_{t+i}|t] = \pi^* = 0, \forall i = \{0, 1, 2, \ldots, \infty\}, \quad (7)$$

where $\pi_{t+i}$ depends on the output gap, $y_{t+i} - z_{t+i}$, according to the New-Keynesian Phillips curve. We assume that information is symmetric. The central bank and market participants share the same information. It follows that the central bank and market participants expect future inflation to be equal to the target rate of zero:

$$\pi^e_{t+1|t} = 0. \quad (8)$$

Normally, it would be important to discuss at this point whether the central bank is able to credibly commit to a policy rule, or whether policy is to be analyzed under the assumption of discretion. However, in the case of a strict-inflation-targeting central bank the optimal policies under commitment and under discretion are identical and follow from the preceding first-order condition.

Solving the Phillips curve for $y_t$ and applying $\pi^e_{t+1|t} = 0$ yields the level of output that would be compatible with the expected rate of inflation in period t:[4]

$$y_t = z_t - \frac{1}{\lambda} u_t. \quad (9)$$

Similarly, the level of output in period t + 1 that would be consistent with optimal policy under current information is given by:

$$y^e_{t+1|t} = z^e_{t+1|t} - \frac{\rho_u}{\lambda} u_t. \quad (10)$$

The appropriate level of the nominal interest rate that achieves the central bank's objective can then be derived from equation (2), the New-Keynesian IS curve, evaluated at the intended levels of output and inflation for periods t and t + 1:

$$z_t - \frac{1}{\lambda} u_t = z^e_{t+1} - \frac{\rho_u}{\lambda} u_t - \varphi (i_t - 0) + g_t. \quad (11)$$

---

[4] Here, steady state inflation $\bar{\pi}$ is normalized at zero consistent with the inflation target.

Thus, the optimal interest rate, $i_t$, is:

$$i_t = \frac{1}{\varphi}\left(z_{t+1|t}^e - z_t + \frac{1 - \rho_u}{\lambda}u_t + g_t\right). \quad (12)$$

This characterization of optimal interest rate policy has several interesting implications regarding the role of money in monetary policy design. As previously stated the monetary aggregate, $m_t$, plays no role in the characterization of optimal interest rate policy. Therefore, improvements in the measurement of monetary aggregates are not likely to improve policy design. Furthermore, the money demand relation, equation (5), is not used in the derivation of the optimal interest rate policy. Thus, money demand parameters do not appear in the optimal policy. Rather, the parameters of the Phillips curve and IS curve turn out to be of importance. This result reinforces the conclusion that research efforts be better spent on obtaining better estimates of the slope of the Phillips curve or the interest-rate elasticity of aggregate demand than estimates of the income and interest-rate elasticities of money demand.

To be clear, the central bank achieves the desired interest rate setting by conducting open-market operations that influence the money supply. Thus, the money supply is determined according to the money demand equation (5) consistently with the desired policy rate, current output and the price level. However, money does not appear as a variable in the central bank's optimal interest rate rule and the remainder of the economy is automatically insulated from money demand shocks. Thus, the case for monetary policy design without money directly follows from the New-Keynesian model.

One difference between the optimal interest rate policy given by equation (12) and the characterizations reported by Clarida et al. (1999) and Rotemberg and Woodford (1997) is the presence of current and expected future po-

tential output, $z_t$ and $z_{t+1}$. This apparent difference is easily reconciled. For example, if potential output equals steady state output one obtains the optimal policy from Clarida et al. (1999):

$$i_t = \frac{1 - \rho_u}{\varphi\lambda}u_t + \frac{1}{\varphi}g_t. \quad (13)$$

It implies that the central bank acts to fully offset the effects of both demand and cost-push shocks on inflation under a strict-inflation targeting regime. In Rotemberg and Woodford (1997) potential output may deviate from steady state output in response to particular shocks. For example, they incorporate government spending and include a government spending shock in place of the demand or preference shock in Clarida et al. (1999). As a result, potential or flexible-price output partly moves with the government spending shock. Furthermore, changes in productivity such as technology shocks are typically assumed to be important drivers of potential output.

A crucial weakness of the above characterization of optimal interest rate policy is that it is not implementable in practice. Neither current potential output, nor future potential output, nor cost-push shocks, nor demand shocks, nor technology shocks are directly observable. All these variables are unknowns that need to be estimated conditional on a particular model of the economy.

This weakness can be addressed by relaxing the assumption of full information on behalf of the central bank and market participants. In doing so we will continue to treat the central bank and market participants symmetrically. In other words, we will continue to assume that they share the same beliefs regarding the appropriate model of the economy.

*Introducing imperfect knowledge*

In the following, we introduce imperfect knowledge regarding economic shocks and unobservable variables such as potential output into the analysis. The superscript $^e$ is used to refer to the central bank's and public's estimates or perceptions. Thus, $z^e_{t|t}$ denotes the central bank's estimate of potential output in period t given the information available at that point in time. Similarly, $u^e_{t|t}$, $g^e_{t|t}$ and $s^e_{t|t}$ refer to the central bank's estimates of these particular economic shocks. We assume that these perceptions represent the best available estimates of the unobservables from the perspective of the central bank. These estimates form the basis for the central bank's forecast of period t inflation, $\pi^e_{t|t} = E[\pi_t|t]$, at the point in period t when it decides on its policy before it can observe the joint consequences of potential output, the cost-push shock and its policy choice on inflation.

Fortunately, the optimal policy under uncertainty can be determined quite easily if the following conditions are fulfilled: The model is linear, the parameters are treated as known and uncertainty is additive. In this case, certainty-equivalence applies. Or in other words, the optimal policy must continue to satisfy the same first-order condition as before, equation (7), with the expectation conditional on the above estimates (see for example Svensson and Woodford (2003) and Wieland (2006)).[5] Thus, the optimal output level in period t is determined similarly to equation (9) but now in expected terms based on the best available estimates of the cost-push shock and current potential output:

$$y^e_{t|t} = z^e_{t|t} - \frac{1}{\lambda} u^e_{t|t}. \qquad (14)$$

The conditions for certainty-equivalence – linearity, known parameters and additive uncertainty – require making important *a-priori* assumptions regarding the processes that determine unobservable variables. Svensson

and Woodford (2003), for example, assume that potential output, $z_t$, in the New-Keynesian model follows an auto-regressive process:

$$z_t = \rho_z z_{t-1} + \varepsilon^z_t, \qquad (15)$$

with known persistence parameter, $\rho_z$, and known variance, $\sigma_{\varepsilon_z}$. This strategy is often employed in studies of optimal policy under uncertainty. Another example is Wieland (2006) who makes a similar assumption regarding the natural rate of unemployment in a model of the Phillips curve with backward- and forward-looking elements.

With regard to the cost-push shock as well as the demand and money-demand shocks, we use another commonly employed assumption. The central bank and market participants only obtain noisy signals denoted by $u^e_t$, $g^e_t$ and $s^e_t$. Thus, the true shocks are related to these signals according to:

$$u_t = u^e_t + \varepsilon^u_t, \qquad (16)$$

$$g_t = g^e_t + \varepsilon^g_t, \qquad (17)$$

$$s_t = s^e_t + \varepsilon^s_t, \qquad (18)$$

where $\varepsilon^u_t$, $\varepsilon^g_t$ and $\varepsilon^s_t$ are Gaussian white noise processes with zero mean and known variances, $\sigma^u_\varepsilon$, $\sigma^g_\varepsilon$ and $\sigma^s_\varepsilon$. Consequently the best estimates of the shocks correspond to $u^e_{t|t} = u^e_t$, $g^e_{t|t} = g^e_t$ and $s^e_{t|t} = s^e_t$.

Given the above-mentioned assumptions the central bank can solve the estimation problem separately from the optimal policy problem. Svensson and Woodford (2003) and Wieland (2006) show how to derive the optimal estimate of potential output, $z^e_{t|t}$, using the Kalman filter. Conditional on this estimate the optimal policy implies setting the nominal

---

[5] Certainty-equivalence fails if multiplicative parameters such as $\lambda$ are unknown. Then, the central bank faces a complex control and estimation problem. Examples are studied by Wieland (2000), Beck and Wieland (2002) and Wieland (2006).

interest rate, $i_t$, so as to achieve the output level defined by (14) in expectation. The appropriate interest rate may be inferred from the IS equation (11). Thus, the optimal policy under imperfect knowledge corresponds to:

$$i_t = \frac{1}{\varphi}\left(z^e_{t+1|t} - z^e_{t|t} + \frac{1-\rho_u}{\lambda}u^e_t + g^e_t\right). \quad (19)$$

Introducing imperfect knowledge per se does not change our earlier conclusions. Optimal interest rate policy is defined without any reference to monetary aggregates. Improved information on money does not help improve the performance of interest rate policy.

As noted previously, the optimal policy depends importantly on the central bank's estimate of potential output, $z_{t|t}$. A possible route for further investigation would be to follow Svensson and Woodford (2003) and Wieland (2006) and study the performance of policy conditional on an *a-priori* assumption concerning the unobservable process of potential output such as equation (15). Clearly, findings obtained in this manner would only be reliable if potential output truly obeys such a process.

Instead, we pursue a different strategy in our further analysis. This strategy follows the influential study of Orphanides (2003). It implies evaluating policy performance for particular scenarios with persistent deviations of the central bank's estimates of potential output from the true values. Orphanides et al. (2000) and Orphanides (2003) showed that historical output gap estimates have been revised repeatedly. The revisions were due to changing views on the appropriate estimate of potential output. Relative to the final estimate of potential output obtained many years later, the Federal Reserve's real-time estimates indicate highly persistent misperceptions.[6] Similar misperceptions occurred in other countries. Gerberding et al. (2006), for example, provide data on German output gap misperceptions. If a central bank relies on such potential output measures in real time policy making, its policy stance may be biased for a sustained period of time.

Thus, we consider the possibility that the central bank and the public may make persistent mistakes in estimating the natural output level – even if they obtain those estimates using all available information conditional on their preferred model and estimation method. The estimate, $z^e_{t|t}$, differs from the true level, $z_t$, to the extent of the misperception, $e_t$:

$$z^e_{t|t} = z_t + e_t. \quad (20)$$

The misperception, $e_t$, affects the final outcomes for aggregate output, money growth and inflation via central bank policy and market participants' expectations. The resulting level of output is given by:

$$y_t = y^e_{t+1|t} - \varphi\left(i_t - \pi^e_{t+1|t}\right) + g_t$$

$$= z^e_{t+1|t} - \frac{\rho_u}{\lambda}u^e_t - \varphi\left(\frac{1}{\varphi}\left(z^e_{t+1|t} - z^e_{t|t} + \frac{1-\rho_u}{\lambda}u^e_t + g^e_t\right) - 0\right) + g_t$$

$$= z_t + e_t - \frac{1}{\lambda}u^e_t + \varepsilon^g_t. \quad (21)$$

If the central bank overestimates potential output by $e_t$, its policy will increase the output

[6] The output gap data for the 1980s and 1990s of Orphanides (2003) was constructed from the Greenbook, the Federal Reserve document summarizing the Board staff's analysis of economic developments distributed to the FOMC members a few days before each FOMC meeting. For the 1960s and 1970s Orphanides could not recover a complete time series for potential output estimates from Federal Reserve sources but notes that discussion of output gap measures appeared in the FOMC Memorandum of Discussion throughout this period. Thus, he uses real-time estimates of potential output that were produced by the Council of Economic Advisers (CEA) in those years and available at FOMC meetings. Orphanides et al. (2000) estimate a worst-case process of misperceptions with a near unit-root (0.96) and standard deviation of 3.77% using quarterly revisions from 1966 to 1994.

gap, $y_t - z_t$, by the same amount $e_t$. As a result, inflation will increase by $\lambda e_t$ over and above the unavoidable fluctuations due to the noise terms $\varepsilon_t^g$ and $\varepsilon_t^u$:

$$\pi_t = \lambda (y_t - z_t) + \beta \pi_{t+1|t}^e + u_t$$

$$= \lambda (z_t + e_t - \frac{1}{\lambda} u_t^e + \varepsilon_t^g - z_t) + \beta * 0 + u_t$$

$$= \lambda e_t + \lambda \varepsilon_t^g + \varepsilon_t^u. \qquad (22)$$

Inflation consequently inherits the persistence properties of the central bank misperceptions. Trend increases or decreases in inflation may therefore be caused by such misperceptions. This point has been made by Orphanides (2003) for the case of a traditional Keynesian-style model with backward-looking expectations formation. In the present chapter and in Beck and Wieland (2008) it is extended to the New-Keynesian model with rational expectations. The next step is to address the request of Lucas (2007) and investigate whether the New-Keynesian model with persistent misperceptions may give a unified account of trends, including trends in monetary aggregates.

## The Long-Run Link Between Money and Inflation and the Consequences of Persistent Central Bank Misperceptions

Researchers and policymakers that are in favor of assigning a special role to money in monetary policy design typically emphasize the long-run link between money and inflation, or in other words, the quantity theory. This long-run relation is consistent with the New-Keynesian model discussed in the preceding section. Taking first differences and re-arranging the money demand equation (5) we

obtain a short-run link between money and inflation:

$$\pi_t = \Delta p_t = \Delta m_t - \gamma_y \Delta y_t + \gamma_i \Delta i_t - \Delta s_t. \quad (23)$$

$\Delta$ is the first-difference operator. Long-run equilibrium values can then be determined as follows. In the long-run, money demand shocks would average to zero, and the nominal interest rate would settle down to its steady state level, which is the sum of the equilibrium real interest rate and the inflation target. Thus, the change in the interest rate would similarly converge to zero. The long-run link between inflation, money growth and output growth then corresponds to:

$$\overline{\pi} = \Delta \overline{m} - \gamma_y \Delta \overline{y} = \overline{\mu}. \qquad (24)$$

This relationship also incorporates the long-run trend in velocity. Thus, long-run inflation is proportional to long-run money growth adjusted for output and velocity trends.[7]

Recent studies obtained empirical support for this long-run relationship by comparing money and inflation trends estimated with different filtering methods.[8] Even more interestingly, they claim that money growth leads inflation at low frequencies. To give an example, Gerlach (2004) uses the following filter:

$$\mu_t^f = \mu_{t-1}^f + \omega (\mu_t - \mu_{t-1}^f), \qquad (25)$$

to approximate long-run values of inflation and money growth. In his work, $\mu_t$, may alternatively stand for money growth, $\Delta m_t$, or money growth adjusted for output growth. In this chapter we adjust money growth as indicated by equation (24) using the estimate of the income-elasticity of money demand, i.e.:

---

[7] Specifically, with velocity defined as $v_t \equiv -m_t + p_t + y_t$ and money demand determined by equation (5) the long-run trend in velocity corresponds to $\Delta \overline{v} = (1 - \gamma_y)\Delta \overline{y}$. Changes in the trend in velocity may arise from changes in potential output growth $\overline{y}$, changes in the income elasticity of money demand, $\gamma_y$, and possibly from other sources such as financial innovations (see Orphanides and Porter (2001) and Masuch et al. (2001)).

[8] See for example Gerlach (2004), Benati (2005), Pill and Rautananen (2006) and Assemacher-Wesche and Gerlach (2007).

$$\mu_t^f = \Delta m_t^f - \gamma_y \Delta y_t^f. \qquad (26)$$

In order to show that introducing persistent central bank misperceptions into the New-Keynesian model is sufficient to generate similar trend movements in money and inflation – the challenge posed by Lucas – we calibrate and simulate the model under imperfect knowledge. The calibrated parameter values are summarized in *Table 1*. The economic parameters ($\beta$, $\varphi$, $\lambda$, $\gamma_y$, $\gamma_i$) are set at values consistent with other studies in the New-Keynesian literature. The variances of the economic shocks are all set to 0.8. The variance of the noise terms is smaller with regard to money than with regard to output and inflation, because monetary data is available earlier at monthly frequency and subject to less revision (see Coenen et al. (2005)). The persistence of the economic shocks, ($\rho_u$, $\rho_g$), is set to zero. The filtering parameter, $\omega$, is set in line with values investigated by Gerlach (2004).

To illustrate the effect of sustained misperceptions we construct a simple example. This particular series of output gap misperceptions measured in percentage point terms was also previously used in Beck and

Wieland (2007a) in the context of a model with backward-looking expectations formation:

$$
\begin{aligned}
&\text{for } t = (1,10) &&e(t) = 0, \\
&\text{for } t = (11,12,13,14) &&e(t) = (1,2,3,4), \\
&\text{for } t = (15,100) &&e(t) = 4, \qquad (27) \\
&\text{for } t = (101,102,103) &&e(t) = (3,2,1), \\
&\text{for } t = (104,200) &&e(t) = 1.
\end{aligned}
$$

The central bank's initial estimate of potential output is assumed to coincide with the true value. In periods 11 to 14 the central bank overestimates potential output growth by 1 percentage point per period. As a consequence, the central bank's and the public's estimate of the output gap is 4 percentage points lower than the true output gap from period 15 onwards. As a result of this mistake the central bank will induce a level of output that is 4 percentage points above potential on average. Ultimately, this policy bias induces an increase in average inflation of about 2 percentage points. This value corresponds to ($\lambda\, e_t$). Accordingly, average money growth will also tend to rise by 2 percentage points. From period 100 onwards the central bank's overestimate of potential output declines to 1 percentage point and the resulting deviation in average inflation to 0.5 percentage points.

*Table 1*

**Calibration**

| PARAMETER | VALUE | ECONOMIC INTERPRETATION |
|---|---|---|
| $\beta$ | 0.99 | Discount factor of the policymaker. |
| $-\varphi$ | −1 | Real interest rate elasticity of aggregate demand (in line with Andres et al. (2006) and Ireland (2004)). |
| $\theta$ | 0.5 | Proportion of firms that adjust prices in a given period (based on Bils and Klenow (2004)). As a result $\lambda = 0.5$ (rounded). |
| $\gamma_y$ | 0.1 | Income elasticity of money demand (in line with Andres et al. (2006) and Ireland (2004)). |
| $-\gamma_i$ | −0.4 | Interest rate elasticity of money demand (in line with Andres et al. (2006) and Ireland (2004)). |
| $\omega$ | 0.2 | Weighting parameter of filter (broadly in line with Gerlach (2004)). |
| $\pi^*$ | 0 | Inflation target. |
| $\rho_u, \rho_g$ | 0 | Persistence of cost-push and aggregate demand shocks. |
| $\sigma_{\eta^\varepsilon}, \sigma_{\eta^u}, \sigma_{\eta^s}$ | 0.8 | Standard deviation of cost-push, demand and money-demand shocks. |
| $\sigma_\varepsilon^u$ | 0.6 | Standard deviation of noise of cost-push shocks. |
| $\sigma_\varepsilon^g$ | 0.4 | Standard deviation of noise of demand shock. |
| $\sigma_\varepsilon^s$ | 0.1 | Standard deviation of noise of money-demand shocks. |

Figure 1
**Output Gap Misperceptions and the Money-Inflation Link**

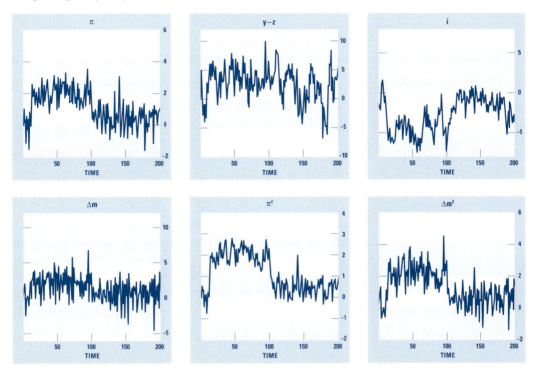

A simulation of the consequences of output gap misperceptions under the optimal policy in the New-Keynesian model is shown in *Figure 1* for a single draw of normally distributed cost-push, demand and money-demand shocks and noise terms. Due to an interest rate policy that is more accommodative than the central bank believes to be the case, money growth and inflation rise. This increase is persistent due to persistent central bank misperceptions regarding potential output. Over time, also the filtered measures of money growth, $\Delta m^f$, and inflation, $\pi^f$, increase. An apparent trend change in nominal variables occurs.

The simulation reported in *Figure 1* suggests that the introduction of imperfect knowledge and persistent central bank misperceptions is sufficient to provide a unified account of

monetary and inflation trends – the unresolved issue on the frontier of macroeconomic theory noted by Robert E. Lucas. Of course, the series of misperceptions simulated above is an ad-hoc choice. However, empirical observations of central bank misperceptions are available for the United States and Germany from Orphanides (2003) and Gerberding et al. (2006). Beck and Wieland (2008) show that these historical misperceptions also generate similar trends in money growth and inflation.

Another potential source of inflation trends that has been considered in empirical estimations of the New-Keynesian model is the inflation target. A common assumption is to model the central bank's inflation target as a random walk. Our explanation based on persistent policy mistakes due to persistent misperceptions regarding unobservables applies in the case of a constant inflation target. It makes use of the empirical observation of persistent output gap revisions and does not require random changes in the central bank's inflation objective.

With regard to the simulation in *Figure 1* one may ask why the central bank does not realize that its perceptions are biased, raises interest rates to a higher level and thereby ensures that inflation returns to target relatively quickly. The reason is simple. Optimal monetary policy takes account of the best available forecast for inflation. This forecast, which is based on an incorrect output gap, states that inflation will return to target due to the belief that aggregate demand is consistent with price stability. If the central bank were to raise interest rates further, its own forecast would indicate a recession and undershooting of its inflation target. The persistent bias in the forecast implies that the central bank is attributing successive periods of high inflation to a sequence of unfavorable shocks rather than a mistaken output gap estimate. This example is not without parallel in reality considering the account of the 1970s inflation in the United States in Orphanides (2003).

## An Interest Rate Policy with Monetary Cross-Checking

Based on the empirical evidence on money growth and inflation trends, Lucas (2007) suggested to continue using information on monetary aggregates as an add-on or cross-check in interest rate policy. In this spirit, we have formulated an interest rate rule with monetary cross-checking in Beck and Wieland (2007a). It consists of two components:

$$i_t = i_t^{NK} + i_t^{CC}. \tag{28}$$

The first component, denoted by the superscript NK, refers to the optimal interest rate policy in the New-Keynesian model as defined by equation (19). The second component, denoted by the superscript CC, refers to an additive adjustment in interest rate setting due to monetary cross-checking.

What is the purpose of having two components? If the central bank believes in the New-Keynesian model, the available information and estimates indicate that $i_t^{NK}$ is the optimal policy choice under uncertainty. In the case of persistent output gap misperceptions, the model-based forecast will indicate that a sequence of inflationary shocks is the source of the observed upward shift in inflation rather than a deviation of output from potential. It is important to understand that this assessment also incorporates information on monetary aggregates. The New-Keynesian model will attribute the upward shift in money growth to the same source. Money is not a neglected information variable. Conditional on the model and the model-consistent output gap estimate money growth does not provide further information affecting the model forecast. The reason is that the level of output and inflation are observed directly. If output, inflation and money growth were afflicted with measurement error, money would provide further information that would help improve estimates of current output and inflation. This information role is investigated by Coenen et al. (2005), but plays no role in the present chapter.

Instead, the idea of cross-checking is motivated from the perspective of model uncertainty and the search for robustness in policy design. The proposal is to base policy on the preferred model in normal times, but to check policy outcomes regularly against another simpler model. In this chapter, the preferred model is the New-Keynesian model of the second section. The simpler model used for cross-checking is the long-run relationship between money and inflation implied by the quantity theory. Of course, as shown in the preceding section, this long-run relationship between money and inflation is part of the New-Keynesian model as well. It is interesting from a robustness perspective, because it also holds in cases where the New-Keynesian model fails, for example, in an economy that is better characterized by a model without price rigidities. Ideally, the regular cross-check should not lead to deviation from the New-Keynesian interest rate policy, $i_t^{NK}$, in normal times, that is in the absence of persistent central bank misperceptions regarding unobservable measures such as the output gap. However, the cross-check should trigger a policy adjustment, $i_t^{CC}$, if trend money growth deviates from a rate consistent with stable inflation in a statistically unusually persistent manner. This statistical test may be based on the null hypothesis that the preferred model is correct.

As shown by Beck and Wieland (2008) the policy with cross-checking can be derived from a first-order condition that includes trend inflation. To illustrate the reasoning we start by reiterating the first-order condition that describes the optimal policy derived under certainty-equivalence:

$$E[\pi_{t+i} - \pi^*|t] = 0 \; \forall i = \{0, 1, 2, \ldots, \infty\}. \quad (29)$$

It implies that trend inflation equals the inflation target in expectation. Specifically, $E[\pi_{t+N}|t] \to E[\bar{\pi}]$ as $N \to \infty$, and consequently $E[\bar{\pi}] = \pi^* = 0$.

Thus, a central bank that relies on the New-Keynesian model expects that trend inflation will turn out to match the target as long as policy is set to stabilize expected inflation

in every period. However, such confidence in model-based forecasts and estimates of unobservable variables may be misplaced. Following Lucas' recommendation, a sceptical policymaker may instead consider a simpler model of trend inflation. A good candidate is the long-run relationship between money and inflation derived from the quantity equation:

$$E[\bar{\pi}] = E[\mu^f]. \quad (30)$$

A "monetarist" central bank that exclusively uses this model of trend inflation to inform policy would conduct open-market operations in period t such that trend inflation as estimated by the most recent observation on filtered adjusted money growth is expected to equal the inflation target:

$$E[\bar{\pi}|\mu_t^f] = \pi^* = 0. \quad (31)$$

$\mu_t^f$ can be monitored without relying on model-based estimates of potential output. As a result, the central bank can stabilize trend inflation in spite of output gap misperceptions.[9]

Clearly, such an approach may appeal to traditional strict monetarists. In our view, however, it would be a mistake to abandon any attempt at short-run inflation stabilization. After all, the New-Keynesian model may not be that far off the mark and potential output estimates need not always be utterly wrong. Instead, we consider the monetary model of trend inflation for cross-checking purposes. Specifically, the central bank is instructed to check every period whether filtered money growth is still consistent with attaining the inflation target or whether trend money growth has shifted. This check is accomplished by monitoring the test statistic:

---

[9] Of course, a natural question concerns the implications of sustained velocity shifts for this strategy of stabilizing trend inflation. This possibility is investigated in Beck and Wieland (2008). There we show that simple recursive estimation of money demand parameters would be effective in avoiding incorrect cross-checks.

$$\kappa_t = \frac{\mu_t^f - \pi^*}{\sigma_{\mu^f}}. \tag{32}$$

and comparing it to a critical value $\kappa^{crit}$. Here, $\sigma_{\mu^f}$ denotes the standard deviation of the filtered money growth measure. It can be determined under the null hypothesis that the central bank's preferred model, that is the New-Keynesian model, is correct.

As long as the test statistic does not signal a sustained shift in filtered money growth, the central bank implements the optimal policy under the preferred Keynesian-style model. This is the policy that satisfies the first-order condition (7). As a result it will stabilize short-run inflation variations very effectively in the absence of persistent output gap misperceptions. Once the central bank receives successive signals of a shift in trend inflation as estimated by filtered money growth, i.e. ($\kappa_t > \kappa^{crit}$ for N periods) or ($\kappa_t < -\kappa^{crit}$ for N periods), policy is adjusted so as to control trend inflation.

The two policy parameters $\kappa^{crit}$ and N play different roles. $\kappa^{crit}$ reflects the probability that an observed deviation of $\mu^f$ from $\pi^*$ is purely accidental (for example a 5% or 1% significance level). N defines the number of successive deviations in excess of this critical value. Thus, the greater N the longer the central bank waits to accumulate evidence of a sustained policy bias. The chosen values are shown in Table 2.

The optimal size of the cross-checking adjustment can be derived from a first-order condition that includes the expectation of trend inflation based on the simple monetary model. It is used to augment the inflation forecast based on the New-Keynesian (NK) model:

$$E[\pi_t | z_{t|t}^e, \text{NK Model}] + E[\overline{\pi} | \mu_t^f] = 0. \tag{33}$$

This condition guarantees that the central bank counteracts a significant shift in trend inflation estimated on the basis of filtered money growth. $\mu_k^f$ denotes the most recent significant estimate of a trend shift in period k, i.e. ($\kappa_k > \kappa^{crit}$, ..., $\kappa_{k-N} > \kappa^{crit}$) or ($\kappa_k < -\kappa^{crit}$, ..., $\kappa_{k-N} < -\kappa^{crit}$).

To derive the interest rate adjustment following a significant cross-check it is important to consider its effect on market participants' expectations of future inflation. Of course, initially neither the central bank nor market participants will expect cross-checking to kick in, because expectations are formed conditional on the New-Keynesian model and the associated estimate of potential output. The probability that the test statistic $\kappa$ exceeds the critical value under the null hypothesis is negligible, and even more so the probability that it exceeds $\kappa^{crit}$ for N periods. Thus, in the absence of a significant cross-check the expectations for inflation in period t under the null hypothesis

*Table 2*

**Parameters of the Cross-Checking Component of Monetary Policy**

| PARAMETER | VALUE | ECONOMIC INTERPRETATION |
|---|---|---|
| $\sigma_{\mu^f}$ | 0.54 | Standard deviation of $\mu^f$ given the calibration of the model equations in *Table 1*. |
| $\kappa^{crit}$ | 1.96 | 5% critical value for the cross-checking rule. |
| N | 4 | Number of periods required for a sustained deviation in the cross-checking rule. |

of the New-Keynesian model and the potential output estimate $z_{t|t}^e$ are given by:

$$\pi_{t|t}^e = 0. \tag{34}$$

Once a significant cross-check occurs, policy is governed by the first-order condition with the monetary estimate of trend inflation from then onwards. As a consequence:

$$\pi_{t|t}^e = -\mu_k^f. \tag{35}$$

Thus, under symmetric information the central bank and market participants will expect current inflation – conditional on the New-Keynesian model and potential output estimate – to fall below the target to the extent of the trend inflation estimate provided by filtered money growth.

To solve the New-Keynesian Phillips curve for the expected output level that the central bank should aim at according to the policy with cross-checking, it is necessary to characterize market participants' expectation of inflation in period $t + 1$. In doing so we focus on the case of policy under discretion. In this case, the central bank cannot manipulate market participants' inflation expectations by promising to commit to delivering future inflation outcomes that are inconsistent with its objective function. Therefore, under discretion market participants expect future inflation to return to the zero inflation target of the central bank, i.e. $\pi_{t+1|t}^e = 0$.

Then, the Phillips curve is solved for the level of output that the central bank expects to achieve in period $t$, $y_{t|t}^e$. Using $\pi_{t+1|t}^e = 0$ and $\pi_{t|t}^e = -\mu_f^k$ one obtains:

$$y_{t|t}^e = z_{t|t}^e + \frac{1}{\lambda}\pi_{t|t}^e - \frac{\beta}{\lambda}\pi_{t+1|t}^e - \frac{1}{\lambda}u_{t|t}^e \tag{36}$$

$$= z_{t|t}^e - \frac{1}{\lambda}u_{t|t}^e - \frac{1}{\lambda}\mu_f^k.$$

Market participants' expectation of output in period $t + 1$ may be characterized in a similar manner. Consistent with the expectation that inflation will be equal to the target in period $t + 1$, market participants expect output to be equal to potential output in period $t + 1$:

$$y_{t+1|t}^e = z_{t+1|t}^e - \frac{\rho_u}{\lambda}u_{t|t}^e. \tag{37}$$

In the next step, the IS curve is solved for the interest rate, $i_t$, consistent with the above expressions for $y_{t|t}^e$, $y_{t+1|t}^e$ and $\pi_{t+1|t}^e$. This yields the interest rate policy with cross-checking:

$$i_t = 0 - \frac{1}{\varphi}\left(z_{t|t}^e - \frac{1}{\lambda}u_{t|t}^e - \frac{1}{\lambda}\mu_f^k\right) +$$
$$\frac{1}{\varphi}\left(z_{t+1|t}^e - \frac{\rho_u}{\lambda}u_{t|t}^e\right) + \frac{1}{\varphi}g_{t|t}^e \tag{38}$$

$$= \frac{1}{\varphi}\left(z_{t+1|t}^e - z_{t|t}^e + \frac{1-\rho_u}{\lambda}u_{t|t}^e + g_{t|t}^e\right) + \frac{1}{\lambda\varphi}\mu_f^k$$

$$= i_t^{NK} + \frac{1}{\lambda\varphi}\mu_f^k. \tag{39}$$

It turns out that the appropriate adjustment to interest rate policy for the periods following a significant cross-check is given by $i_t^{CC} = \frac{1}{\lambda\varphi}\mu_f^k$. The dynamic characterization of interest rate policy then corresponds to:

$$i_t = \begin{cases} i_t^{NK} + \left(\frac{1}{\varphi\lambda}\right)\left(\mu_k^f\right) & \text{if} \quad (\kappa_t > \kappa^{crit}, \ldots, \kappa_{t-N} > \kappa^{crit}) \\ & \text{or} \quad (\kappa_t < -\kappa^{crit}, \ldots, \kappa_{t-N} < -\kappa^{crit}) \\ i_t^{NK} + 0 & \text{else.} \end{cases} \tag{40}$$

Next, we aim to show that the interest rate policy with cross-checking provides a convenient and effective avenue for correcting the central bank's policy bias that led to the sustained increase in filtered money growth and inflation in the preceding simulation. To this end, we repeat the simulation of *Figure 1* using the policy defined by equation (40). The outcome is reported in *Figure 2*. The panel with actual money growth, $\Delta m$, is omitted. Instead we include a panel reporting the misperception in the central bank's estimate of potential output, $e_t$, and the adjustment in interest rates due to monetary cross-checking, $i_t^{CC}$.

The policy with cross-checking responds to the increase in filtered money growth, $\mu_t^f$, fairly quickly after the policy bias has arisen. The interest rate adjustment of $\left(\frac{1}{\lambda\varphi}\right)\left(\mu_k^f\right)$

almost perfectly offsets the policy bias due to the output gap misperception, $(e_t)$. Once the misperception of potential output declines after period 100 cross-checking soon leads to another adjustment of interest rates.

To assess the sensitivity of our findings we draw 1000 series of shocks of 200 periods length from a normal distribution and use them to conduct a set of alternative simulations. Some of the findings are reported in *Figure 3*. The bottom right panel of *Figure 3* reports the average path of the interest rate adjustment due to monetary cross-checking, i.e. $i_t^{CC}$, over 1000 simulations under the same parameter settings as in the single simulation displayed in *Figure 2*. This panel confirms that, on average, cross-checking leads to the appropriate interest rate adjustments offsetting the policy bias due to output gap misperceptions.

*Figure 2*

**Output Gap Misperceptions and Monetary Cross-Checking**

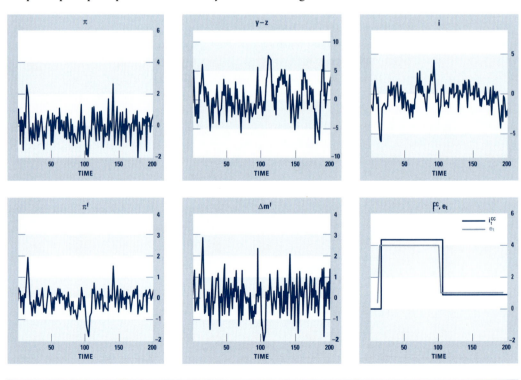

*Figure 3*

**Sensitivity Analysis: Averages over 1000 Simulations**

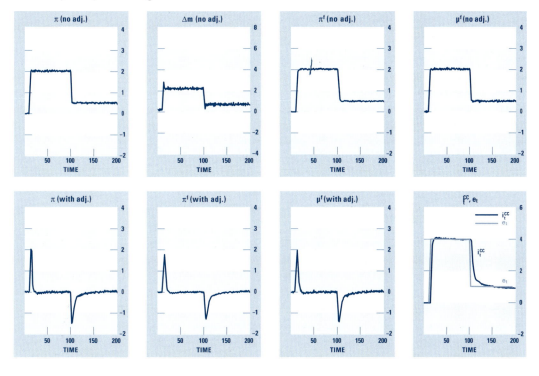

## Conclusions and Outlook

In this chapter, we have presented the case for monetary policy without money in the New-Keynesian model. This analysis supports Michael Woodford's conclusion that monetary aggregates do not play an important role in optimal interest rate policy. Furthermore, we have shown that the empirical observation of similar trends in money growth and inflation is not in itself a reason to discard the New-Keynesian model. Similar long-run trends of money growth and inflation can be explained within the New-Keynesian model. Our analysis indicates that such trends would emerge as a consequence of a sustained policy bias. A possible source of this bias are persistent central bank misperceptions regarding unobservable potential output. Empirical evidence on the existence of such misperceptions is available for the United States and Germany.

Nevertheless, we find that monetary aggregates can play a useful role in designing a robust monetary policy strategy. In particular, it may be useful to augment the optimal model-based interest rate policy with a monetary cross-check if the central bank's model-based estimates of unobservables such as potential output embody persistent misperceptions. Such a cross-check can help correcting the policy bias due to misperceptions by adding an adjustment to the interest rate prescription from the central bank's preferred New-Keynesian model that is derived from a money-based estimate of trend inflation. This adjustment would not be made in normal times, but only when the money-based estimate of trend inflation has deviated in an unusual and persistent manner from target. The optimal interest policy prescription from the preferred New-Keynesian model does not adjust automatically, because the central bank's output gap estimate and model-based forecast interpret the change in inflation simply as the outcome of a particularly unfavorable series of shocks.

In Beck and Wieland (2007a,b) we have noted the similarity between monetary cross-checking as defined above and the ECB's claim that it bases its interest-rate decisions on a strategy with two main components or pillars. In particular, the ECB's strategy is not exclusively focused on short- to medium-run determinants of inflation, but also includes a separate, long-run oriented monetary analysis. In the ECB website these two components are described as follows:

*"**Economic analysis** assesses the short to medium-term determinants of price developments. The focus is on real activity and financial conditions in the economy. The economic analysis takes account of the fact that price developments over those horizons are influenced largely by the interplay of supply and demand in the goods, services and factor markets."*

*"**Monetary analysis** focuses on a longer-term horizon than the economic analysis. It exploits the long-run link between money and prices. The monetary analysis mainly serves as a means of cross-checking, from a medium to long-term perspective, the short to medium-term indications for monetary policy coming from the economic analysis."*

We are tempted to associate the ECB's "economic analysis" with the optimal interest rate policy derived from the New-Keynesian model, denoted by $i_t^{NK}$ in this chapter. Our reasoning for this association is that this setting of the interest rate will ensure that short- to medium-run inflationary risks based on a forward-looking Phillips curve and excess aggregate demand are perfectly controlled. Similarly, we are tempted to associate the ECB's "monetary analysis" with the cross-checking adjustment, denoted by $i_t^{CC}$. As outlined in the preceding section this adjustment exploits the long-run link between money and prices. However, we note that the ECB has refrained from providing a formal quantitative exposition of the conduct and combination of its "economic" and "monetary" analysis. Therefore, this association remains speculative and in need of further empirical investigation.

Our definition of a policy with cross-checking would also allow incorporating cross-checks regarding other estimates of trend inflation. While the quantity theory suggests filtered money growth as an obvious candidate, past measures of filtered inflation would work as well (see Beck and Wieland (2008)). However, those staff in charge of inflation forecasting may be reluctant to insist on an additional policy response to past inflation that would lead them to predict an under- or over-shooting of inflation conditional on the preferred model of inflation. For this reason, one could also speculate whether such an insistence on reacting to past outcomes is perhaps better incorporated in the context of a long-run monetary analysis conducted separately from those in charge of short-run inflation forecasting in a central bank.

# REFERENCES

**Andrés, J., J. D. López-Salido, and J. Vallés.** 2006. "Money in an estimated business cycle model of the euro area." *Economic Journal*, 116: 457–477.

**Assenmacher-Wesche, K., and S. Gerlach.** 2007. "Interpreting euro area inflation at high and low frequencies." *Journal of the European Economic Assocation*, 5: 534–542.

**Beck, G. W., and V. Wieland.** 2002. "Learning and control in a changing economic environment." *Journal of Economic Dynamics and Control*, 26(9-10): 1359–1377.

**Beck, G. W., and V. Wieland.** 2007a. "Money in monetary policy design: A formal characterization of ECB-style crosschecking." *Journal of the European Economic Association*, 5: 524–533.

**Beck, G. W., and V. Wieland.** 2007b. "Money in monetary policy design: The two-pillar Phillips curve versus ECB-style cross-checking." Center for Economic Policy Research Discussion Paper 6098.

**Beck, G. W., and V. Wieland.** 2008. "Central bank misperceptions and the role of money in interest rate rules." *Journal of Monetary Economics*, 55S: S1–S18.

**Benati, L.** 2005. "Long-run evidence on money growth and inflation." Bank of England Quarterly Bulletin.

**Bils, M., and P. Klenow.** 2004. "Some evidence on the importance of sticky prices." *Journal of Political Economy*, 112: 987–985.

**Christiano, L. J., and M. Rostagno.** 2001. "Money growth monitoring and the Taylor rule." National Bureau of Economic Research Working Paper 8539.

**Clarida, R., J. Galí, and M. Gertler.** 1999. "The science of monetary policy: A new Keynesian perspective." *Journal of Economic Literature*, XXXVII: 1661–1701.

**Coenen, G., A. T. Levin, and V. Wieland.** 2005. "Data uncertainty and the role of money as an information variable for monetary policy." *European Economic Review*, 49: 975–1006.

**Gerberding, C., F. Seitz, and A. Worms.** 2006. "Monetary policy and real-time data: The case of Europe, Asia and the US." In *Integration in Asia and Europe: Historical Dynamics, Political Issues, and Economic Perspectives*, ed. P. Welfens, F. Knipping, S. Chirathivat and C. Ryan, 165–182. Springer.

**Gerlach, S.** 2004. "The two pillars of the European Central Bank." *Economic Policy*, 40: 389–439.

**Goodfriend, M. and R. King.** 1997. "The Neoclassical Synthesis and the Role of Monetary Policy." In *NBER macroeconomics annual 1997*, ed. B. S. Bernanke and J. J. Rotemberg, 231-83. Cambridge, MA: MIT Press.

**Ireland, P. N.** 2004. "Money's role in the monetary business cycle." *Journal of Money, Credit and Banking*, 36: 969–983.

**Kerr, W., and R. G. King.** 1996. "Limits on interest rate rules in the IS model." Economic Quarterly, Federal Reserve Bank of Richmond, issue Spr, 47-75.

**Lucas, Jr., R. E.** 2007. "Central banking: Is science replacing art?" In *Monetary Policy: A Journey From Theory to Practice*, European Central Bank.

**Orphanides, A.** 2003. "The quest for prosperity without inflation." *Journal of Monetary Economics*, 50: 633–663.

**Orphanides, A., R. D. Porter, D. Reifschneider, R. J. Tetlow, and F. Finan.** 2000. "Errors in the measurement of the output gap and the design of monetary policy." *Journal of Economics and Business*, 52: 117–141.

**Pill, H., and T. Rautananen.** 2006. "Monetary analysis – the ECB experience." Paper presented at the conference "The ECB and its Watchers VIII", May 5, 2006.

**Rotemberg, J., and M. Woodford.** 1997. "An optimization-based econometric framework for the evaluation of monetary policy." In *NBER macroeconomics annual 1997*, ed. B. S. Bernanke and J. J. Rotemberg, 297-346.

**Svensson, L. E. O.** 1997. "Inflation forecast targeting: Implementing and monitoring inflation targets." *European Economic Review*, 41: 1111–1146.

**Svensson, L. E. O., and M. Woodford.** 2003. "Indicator variables for optimal policy." *Journal of Monetary Economics*, 50: 691–720.

**Wieland, V.** 2000. "Learning by doing and the value of optimal experimentation." *Journal of Economic Dynamics and Control*, 24(4): 501-534.

**Wieland, V.** 2006. "Monetary policy and uncertainty about the natural unemployment rate: Brainard-style conservatism versus experimental action." *Advances in Macroeconomics*, 6(1).

**Woodford, M.** 2003. *Interest and Prices: Foundations of a Theory of Monetary Policy*. Princeton, NJ: Princeton University Press.

**Woodford, M.** 2006. "How important is money in the conduct of monetary policy?" Paper prepared for the Fourth ECB Central Banking Conference, The Role of Money: Money and Monetary Policy in the Twenty-First Century.

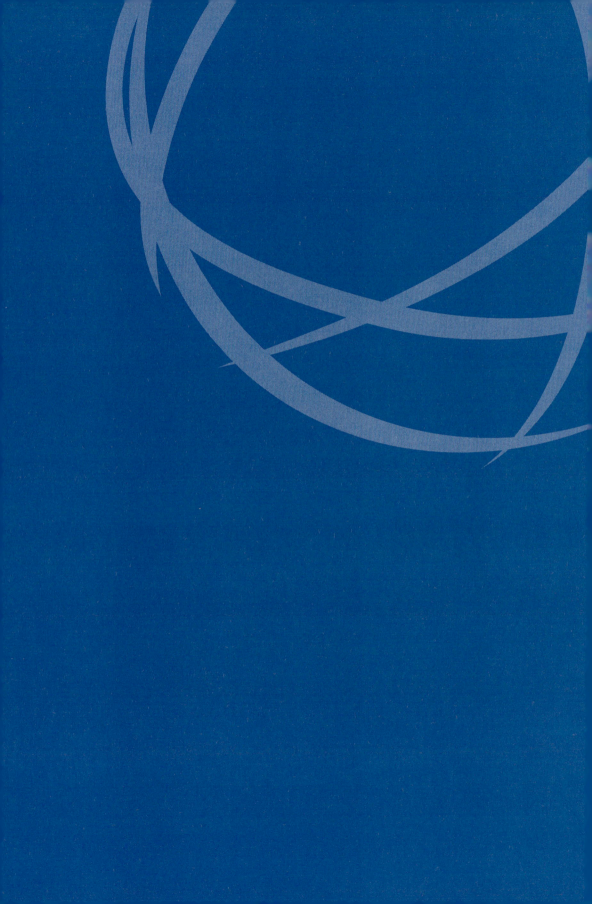

# WILL MONETARY POLICY
# BECOME MORE OF A SCIENCE?

# WILL MONETARY POLICY BECOME MORE OF A SCIENCE?*

**Frederic S. Mishkin (Federal Reserve Board)****

Over the past three decades, we have seen a remarkable change in the performance of monetary policy. By the end of the 1970s, inflation had risen to very high levels, with many countries in the Organisation for Economic Co-operation and Development (OECD) experiencing double-digit inflation rates (*Figure 1*). Most OECD countries today have inflation rates around the 2 percent level, which is consistent with what most economists see as price stability, and the volatility of inflation has also fallen dramatically (*Figure 2*). One concern might be that the low and stable levels of inflation might have been achieved at the expense of higher volatility in output, but that is not what has occurred. Output volatility has also declined in most OECD countries (*Figure 3*). The improved performance of monetary policy has been associated with advances in the science of monetary policy, that is, a set of principles that have been developed from rigorous theory and empirical work that have come to guide the thinking of monetary policy practitioners.

In this chapter, I will review the progress that the science of monetary policy has made over recent decades. In my view, this progress has significantly expanded the degree to which the practice of monetary policy reflects the application of a core set of "scientific" principles. Does this progress mean that, as Keynes put it, monetary policy will become as boring as dentistry – i.e., that policy will be reduced to the routine application of core principles, much like filling cavities?[1] I will argue that there remains, and will likely always remain, elements of art in the conduct of monetary policy; in other words, substantial judgment will always be needed to achieve desirable outcomes on both the inflation and employment fronts.

* Paper first published in *Monetary Policy Over Fifty Years: Experiences and Lessons*, June 2nd 2009, Routledge.

** The views expressed here are my own and are not necessarily these of the Board of Governors or the Federal Reserve System. I thank Michael Kiley, Andrew Levin, and Robert Tetlow for their helpful comments and assistance.

[1] Given that my wife was a dentist, I have to say that Keynes may have been unfair to dentists. I am sure that many of them find their work very exciting.

*Figure 1*

**Headline Inflation**

* Inflation measured by RPI index.

** Inflation measured by national consumer price index.

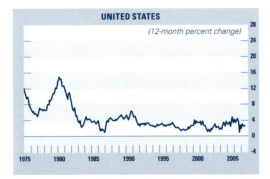

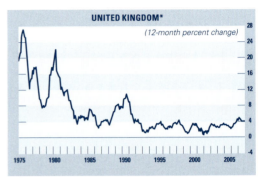

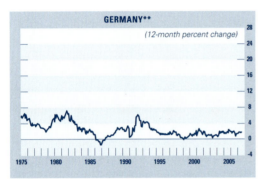

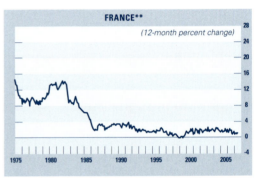

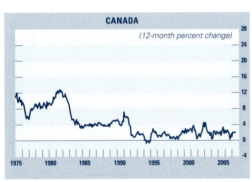

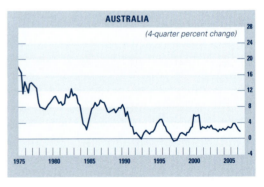

## Advances in the Science of Monetary Policy in Recent Decades

Over the last five decades, monetary economists have developed a set of basic scientific principles, derived from theory and empirical evidence that now guide thinking at almost all central banks and explain much of the success in the conduct of monetary policy. I will outline my views on the key principles and how they were developed over the last fifty or so years.

## The principles are:

1. *Inflation is always and everywhere a monetary phenomenon;*
2. *price stability has important benefits;*
3. *there is no long-run trade-off between unemployment and inflation;*
4. *expectations play a crucial role in the determination of inflation and in the transmission of monetary policy to the macroeconomy;*
5. *real interest rates need to rise with higher inflation, i.e., the Taylor Principle;*
6. *monetary policy is subject to the time-inconsistency problem;*
7. *central bank independence helps improve the efficiency of monetary policy;*
8. *commitment to a strong nominal anchor is central to producing good monetary policy outcomes; and*
9. *financial frictions play an important role in business cycles.*

I will examine each principle in turn.

## Inflation is Always and Everywhere a Monetary Phenomenon

By the 1950s and 1960s, the majority of macroeconomists had converged on a consensus view of macroeconomic fluctuations that downplayed the role of monetary factors. Much of this consensus reflected the aftermath of the Great Depression and Keynes' seminal *The General Theory of Employment, Interest, and Prices*, which emphasized shortfalls in aggregate demand as the source of the Great Depression and the role of fiscal factors as possible remedies. In contrast, research by Milton Friedman and others in what became known as the "monetarist" tradition (Friedman and Meiselman 1963; Friedman and Schwartz 1963a, b) attributed much of the economic malaise of the great Depression to poor monetary policy decisions and more generally argued that the growth in the money supply was a key determinant of aggregate economic activity and, particularly, inflation. Over time, this research, as well as Friedman's predictions that expansionary monetary policy in the 1960s would lead to high inflation and high interest rates (Friedman 1968), had a major impact on the economics profession, with almost all economists eventually coming to agree with the Friedman's famous adage, "Inflation is always and everywhere a monetary phenomenon" (Friedman 1963 p. 17), as long as inflation is referring to a sustained increase in the price level (e.g., Mishkin 2007a).

General agreement with Friedman's adage did not mean that all economists subscribed to the view that the money growth was the most informative piece of information about inflation, but rather that the ultimate source of inflation was overly expansionary monetary policy. In particular, an important imprint of this line of thought was that central bankers came to recognize that keeping inflation under control was their responsibility.[2]

---

[2] Furthermore, monetarist research led Keynesian economists – for example Franco Modigliani – to search for transmission mechanisms linking monetary policy to output and inflation (Mishkin 2007a, chapter 23).

*Figure 2*

**Standard Deviation of Headline Inflation
(5-year window)**

* Inflation measured by RPI index.

** Inflation measured by national consumer price index.

UNITED STATES
(Standard deviation)

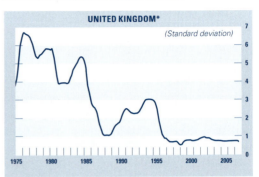

UNITED KINGDOM*
(Standard deviation)

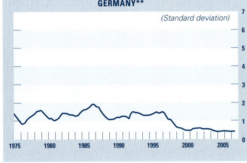

GERMANY**
(Standard deviation)

FRANCE**
(Standard deviation)

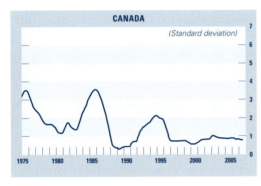

CANADA
(Standard deviation)

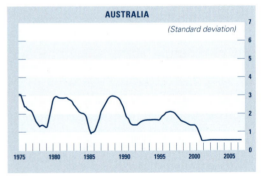

AUSTRALIA
(Standard deviation)

SWEDEN
(Standard deviation)

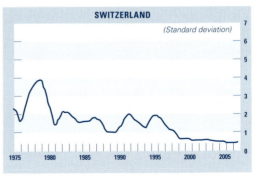

SWITZERLAND
(Standard deviation)

*Figure 3*

**Standard Deviation of Output Growth (5-year window)**

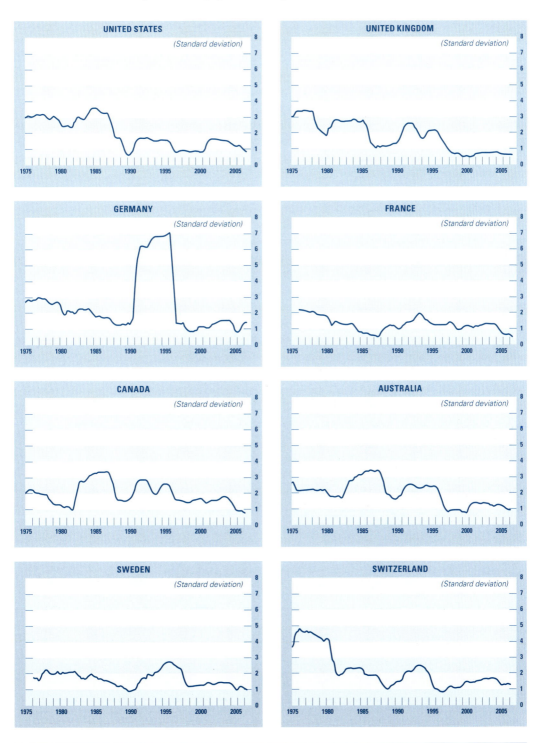

## The Benefits of Price Stability

With the rise of inflation in the 1960s and 1970s, economists, and also the public and politicians, began to discuss the high costs of inflation (for example, see the surveys in Fischer 1993; and Anderson and Gruen 1995). High inflation undermines the role of money as a medium of exchange by acting as a tax on cash holdings. On top of this, a high-inflation environment leads to overinvestment in the financial sector, which expands to help individuals and businesses escape some of the costs of inflation (English 1996). Inflation leads to uncertainty about relative prices and the future price level, making it harder for firms and individuals to make appropriate decisions, thereby decreasing economic efficiency (Lucas 1972; Briault 1995). The interaction of the tax system and inflation also increases distortions that adversely affect economic activity (Feldstein 1997). Unanticipated inflation causes redistributions of wealth, and, to the extent that high inflation tends to be associated with volatile inflation, these distortions may boost the costs of borrowing. Finally, some households undoubtedly do not fully understand the implications of a general trend in prices – that is, they may suffer from nominal illusion – making financial planning more difficult.[3] The total effect of these distortions became more fully appreciated over the course of the 1970s, and the recognition of the high costs of inflation led to the view that low and stable inflation can increase the level of resources productively employed in the economy.[4] [5]

## No Long-Run Trade-off Between Unemployment and Inflation

A paper published in 1960 by Samuelson and Solow argued that work by Phillips (1958), which became known as the Phillips curve, suggested that there was a long-run trade-off between unemployment and inflation and that this trade-off should be exploited. Under this view, the policymaker would have to choose between two competing goals – inflation and unemployment – and decide how high an inflation rate he or she would be willing to accept to attain a lower unemployment rate. Indeed, Samuelson and Solow even mentioned that a nonperfectionist goal of a 3 percent unemployment rate could be achieved at what they considered to be a not-too-high inflation rate of 4 percent to 5 percent per year. This thinking was influential, and probably contributed to monetary and fiscal policy activism aimed at bringing the economy to levels of employment that, with hindsight, were not sustainable. Indeed, the economic record from the late 1960s through the 1970s was not a happy one: Inflation accelerated, with the inflation rate in the United States and other industrialized countries eventually climbing above 10 percent in the 1970s, leading to what has been dubbed "The Great Inflation."

The trade-off suggested by Samuelson and Solow was hotly contested by Friedman (1968) and Phelps (1968), who independently argued that there was no long-run trade-off between unemployment and the inflation rate: Rather, the economy would gravitate to some natural rate of unemployment in the long-run no matter what the rate of inflation was. In other

---

[3] Of course, economic theory implies that inflation can be either too high or too low. The discussion has emphasized costs associated with high inflation. But there are also potentially important costs associated with rates of inflation that are very low. For example, Akerlof, Dickens, and Perry (1996) suggest that downward nominal wage rigidity could result in severe difficulties for economic performance at some times when inflation is too low. Other research has shown that the zero lower bound on nominal interest rates can lower economic efficiency if inflation is too low (e.g. Reifschneider and Williams 2000). Eggertsson and Woodford (2003) discuss strategies to address the zero-lower-bound problem.

[4] A further possibility is that low inflation may even help increase the rate of economic growth. While time-series studies of individual countries and cross-national comparisons of growth rates were not in total agreement (Anderson and Gruen 1995), the consensus grew that inflation is detrimental to economic growth, particularly when inflation rates are high.

[5] The deleterious effects of inflation on economic efficiency implies that the level of sustainable employment is probably lower at higher rates of inflation. Thus, the goals of price stability and high employment are likely to be complementary, rather than competing, and so there is no policy trade-off between the goals of price stability and maximum sustainable employment, the so-called dual mandate that the Federal Reserve has been given by Congress (Mishkin 2007b).

words, the long-run Phillips curve would be vertical, and attempts to lower unemployment below the natural rate would result only in higher inflation. The Friedman-Phelps natural rate hypothesis was immediately influential and fairly quickly began to be incorporated in formal econometric models.

Given the probable role that the attempt to exploit a long-run Phillips curve trade-off had in the "Great Inflation," central bankers have been well served by adopting the natural rate, or no-long-run trade-off, view. Of course, the earlier discussion of the benefits of price stability suggests a long-run trade-off – but not of the Phillips curve type. Rather, low inflation likely contributes to improved efficiency and hence higher employment in the long-run.

## The Crucial Role of Expectations

A key aspect of the Friedman-Phelps natural rate hypothesis was that sustained inflation may initially confuse firms and households, but in the long-run sustained inflation would not boost employment because *expectations* of inflation would adjust to any sustained rate of increase in prices. Starting in the early 1970s, the rational expectations revolution, launched in a series of papers by Lucas (1972, 1973, and 1976), took this reasoning a step further and demonstrated that the public and the markets' expectations

of policy actions have important effects on almost every sector of the economy.[6] The theory of rational expectations emphasized that economic agents should be driven by optimizing behavior, and therefore their expectations of future variables should be optimal forecasts (the best guess of the future) using all available information. Because the optimizing behavior posited by rational expectations indicates that expectations should respond immediately to new information, rational expectations suggests that the long-run might be quite short, so that attempting to lower unemployment below the natural rate could lead to higher inflation very quickly.

A fundamental insight of the rational expectations revolution is that expectations about future monetary policy have an important impact on the evolution of economic activity. As a result, the systematic component of policymakers' actions – i.e., the component that can be anticipated – plays a crucial role in the conduct of monetary policy. Indeed, the management of expectations about future policy has become a central element of monetary theory, as emphasized in the recent synthesis of Woodford (2003).[7] And this insight has far-reaching implications, for example, with regard to the types of systematic behavior by policymakers that are likely to be conducive to macroeconomic stability and growth.[8]

---

[6] The 1976 Lucas paper was already very influential in 1973, when it was first presented at the Carnegie-Rochester Conference. Note that although Muth (1961) introduced the idea of rational expectations more than ten years earlier, his work went largely unnoticed until resurrected by Lucas.

[7] Indeed, one implication of rational expectations in a world of flexible wages and prices was the policy ineffectiveness proposition, which indicated that if monetary policy was anticipated, it would have no real effect on output; only unanticipated monetary policy could have a significant impact. Although evidence for the policy ineffectiveness proposition turned out to be weak (Barro 1977; Mishkin 1982a, b, 1983), the rational expectation revolution's point that monetary policy's impact on the economy is substantially influenced by whether it is anticipated or not has become widely accepted.

[8] Of course, the recognition that management of expectations is a central element in monetary policymaking raises to the forefront the credibility of monetary policy authorities to do what they say they will do. It does not diminish, however, the importance of actions by the monetary authorities because "actions speak louder than words": Monetary authorities will be believed only if they take the actions consistent with how they want expectations to be managed.

## The Taylor Principle

The recognition that economic outcomes depend on expectations of monetary policy suggests that policy evaluation requires the comparison of economic performance under different monetary policy rules.[9] One type of rule that has received enormous attention in the literature is the Taylor rule (Taylor 1993a), which describes monetary policy as setting an overnight bank rate in response to the deviation of inflation from its desired level or target (the inflation gap) and the deviation of output from its natural rate level (the output gap).[10] Taylor (1993a) emphasized that a rule of this type had desirable properties and in particular would stabilize inflation only if the coefficient on the inflation gap exceeded unity. This conclusion came to be known as the "Taylor principle" (Woodford 2001) and can be described most simply by saying that stabilizing monetary policy must raise the nominal interest rate by more than the rise in inflation. In other words, inflation will remain under control only if real interest rates rise in response to a rise in inflation. Although, the Taylor principle now seems pretty obvious, estimates of Taylor rules, such as those by Clarida, Galí, and Gertler (1998), indicate that during the late 1960s and 1970s many central banks, including the Federal Reserve, violated the Taylor principle, resulting in the "Great Inflation" that so many countries experienced during this period.[11] Indeed, as inflation rose in the United States, real interest rates fell.[12]

## The Time-Inconsistency Problem

Another important development in the science of monetary policy that emanated from the rational expectations revolutions was the discovery of the importance of the time-inconsistency problem in papers by Kydland and Prescott (1977), Calvo (1978), and Barro and Gordon (1983). The time-inconsistency problem can arise if monetary policy conducted on a discretionary, day-by-day basis leads to worse long-run outcomes than could be achieved by committing to a policy rule. In particular, policymakers may find it tempting to exploit a short-run Phillips curve trade-off between inflation and employment; but private agents, cognizant of this temptation, will adjust expectations to anticipate the expansionary policy, so that it will result only in higher inflation with no short-run increase in employment. In other words, without a commitment mechanism, monetary policymakers may find themselves unable to *consistently* follow an optimal plan over time; the optimal plan can be *time-inconsistent* and so will soon be abandoned. The notion of time-inconsistency has led to a number of important insights regarding central bank behavior – such as the importance of reputation (formalized in the concept of *reputational equilibria*) and institutional design.

---

[9] Although Lucas (1976) was a critique of the then-current practice of using econometric models to evaluate specific policy actions, it leads to the conclusion that monetary policy analysis should involve the comparison of economic performance arising from different rules.

[10] Variants of the Taylor rule also allow for interest rate smoothing, as in Taylor (1999).

[11] In contrast, Orphanides (2003) argues that the Federal Reserve did abide by the Taylor principle but pursued overly expansionary policies during this period because of large and persistent misperceptions of the level of potential output and the natural unemployment rate.

[12] E.g. the estimates in Mishkin (1981, 1992).

## Central Bank Independence

Indeed, the potential problem of time-inconsistency has led to a great deal of research that examines the importance of institutional features that can give central bankers the commitment mechanisms they need to pursue low inflation. Perhaps the most significant has been research showing that central bank independence, at least along some dimensions, is likely very important to maintaining low inflation. Allowing central banks to be instrument independent, i.e., to control the setting of monetary policy instruments, can help insulate them from short-run pressures to exploit the Phillips-curve trade-off between employment and inflation and thus avoid the time-inconsistency problem.[13]

Evidence supports the conjecture that macroeconomic performance is improved when central banks are more independent. When central banks in industrialized countries are ranked from least legally independent to most legally independent, the inflation performance is found to be the best for countries with the most independent central banks (Alesina and Summers 1993; Cukierman 1993; Fischer 1994; and the surveys in Forder 2000, and Cukierman 2006).

A particularly interesting example occurred with the granting of instrument independence to the Bank of England in May of 1997 (Mishkin and Posen 1997; Bernanke et al. 1999); before that date, the Chancellor of the Exchequer set the monetary policy instrument, not the Bank of England. As *Figure 4* illustrates, during 1995-96 the U.K. retail inflation rate (RPIX) was fairly close to 3 percent, but the spread between nominal and indexed bond yields – referred to as 10-year breakeven inflation – was substantially higher, in the range of 4 percent to 5 percent, reflecting investors' inflation expectations as well as compensation for perceived inflation risk at a 10-year horizon. Notably, breakeven inflation declined markedly on the day that the government announced the Bank of England's independence and has remained substantially lower ever since. This case study provides a striking example of the benefits of instrument independence.

Although there is a strong case for instrument independence, the same is not true for goal independence, the ability of the central bank to set its own goals for monetary policy.[14] In a democracy, the public exercises control over government actions, and policymakers are accountable, which requires that the goals of monetary policy be set by the elected government. Although basic democratic principles argue for the government setting the goals of monetary policy, the question of whether it should set goals for the short-run or intermediate-run is more controversial. For example, an arrangement in which the government set a short-run inflation or exchange rate target that was changed every month or every quarter could easily lead to a serious time-inconsistency problem in which short-run objectives would dominate. In practice, however, this problem does not appear to be severe because, for example, in many countries in which the government sets the annual inflation target, the target is rarely changed once price stability is achieved. Even though, in theory, governments could manipulate monetary policy goals to pursue short-run objectives, they usually do not if the goal-setting process is highly transparent.

---

[13] For an example of how the time-inconsistency problem can be modeled as resulting from political pressure, see Mishkin and Westelius (forthcoming). Instrument independence also insulates the central bank from the myopia that can be a feature of the political process. Instrument independence thus makes it more likely that the central bank will be forward looking and adequately allow for the long lags from monetary policy actions to inflation in setting their policy instruments.

[14] The distinction between goal and instrument independence was first made by Debelle and Fischer (1994) and Fischer (1994).

Figure 4
**Inflation Compensation 10 Years Ahead**

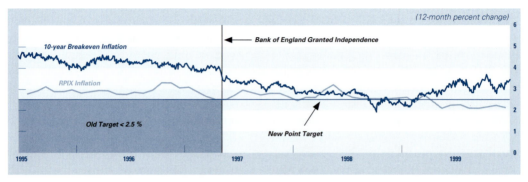

**Notes:** RPI series is not seasonally adjusted; breakeven inflation uses a real bond indexed to RPI inflation.

However, the length of the lags from monetary policy to inflation is a technical issue that the central bank is well placed to determine. Thus, for example, deciding how long it should take for inflation to return to a long-run goal necessarily requires judgment and expertise regarding the nature of the inflation process and its interaction with real activity.

That need for judgment and expertise argues for having the central bank set medium-term goals because the speed with which it can achieve them depends on the lags of monetary policy. Whether the central bank or the government should set medium-term inflation targets is therefore an open question.

## Commitment to a Nominal Anchor

The inability of monetary policy to boost employment in the long-run, the importance of expectations, the benefits of price stability, and the time-inconsistency problem are the reasons that commitment to a nominal anchor – i.e., stabilization of a nominal variable such as the inflation rate, the money supply, or an exchange rate – is crucial to successful monetary policy outcomes.

An institutional commitment to price stability via establishing a nominal anchor provides a counterbalance to the time-inconsistency problem because it makes it clear that the central bank must focus on the long-run and thus resist the temptation to pursue short-run expansionary policies that are inconsistent with the nominal anchor. Commitment to a nominal anchor can also encourage the government to be more fiscally responsible, which also supports price stability. For example, persistent fiscal imbalances have, in the absence of a strong nominal anchor, led some governments, particularly in less-developed economies, to resort to the so-called inflation tax – the printing and issuing of money to pay for goods and services that leads to more inflation and is thus inconsistent with price stability.

Commitment to a nominal anchor also leads to policy actions that promote price stability, which helps promote economic efficiency and growth. The commitment to a nominal anchor helps stabilize inflation expectations, which reduce the likelihood of "inflation scares," in which expected inflation and interest rates shoot up (Goodfriend 1993). Inflation scares lead to bad economic outcomes because the rise in inflation expectations leads not only to higher actual inflation but also to monetary policy tightening to get inflation back under control that often results in large declines in economic activity. Commitment to a nominal anchor is therefore a crucial element in the successful management of expectations; and it is a key feature of recent theory on optimal monetary policy, referred to as the new-neoclassical (or New-Keynesian) synthesis (Goodfriend and King 1997; Clarida, Galí, and Gertler 1999; Woodford 2003). A successful commitment to a nominal anchor has been found to produce not only more-stable inflation but lower volatility of output fluctuations (Fatás, Mihov, and Rose 2007; Mishkin and Schmidt-Hebbel 2002, 2007).

## Financial Frictions and the Business Cycle

Research that outlined how asymmetric information could impede the efficient functioning of the financial system (Akerlof 1970; Myers and Majluf 1984; Greenwald, Stiglitz, and Weiss 1984) suggests an important link between business cycle fluctuations and financial frictions. When shocks to the financial system increase information asymmetry so that financial frictions increase dramatically, financial instability results, and the financial system is no longer able to channel funds to those with productive investment opportunities, with the result that the economy can experience a severe economic downturn (Mishkin 1997). The rediscovery of Irving Fisher's (1933) paper on the Great Depression led to the recognition that financial instability played a central role in the collapse of economic activity during that period (Mishkin 1978; Bernanke,1983; and the survey in Calomiris 1993), and it has spawned a large literature on the role of financial frictions in business cycle fluctuations (e.g., Bernanke and Gertler 1999, 2001; Bernanke, Gertler, and Gilchrist 1999; Kashyap and Stein 1994). Indeed, it is now well understood that the most severe business cycle downturns are always

associated with financial instability, not only in advanced countries but also in emerging-market countries (Mishkin 1991, 1996). Minimizing output fluctuations thus requires that monetary policy factors in the impact of financial frictions on economic activity.

## Advances in the Applied Science of Monetary Policy

Scientific principles are all well and good, but they have to be applied in a practical way to produce good policies. The scientific principles from physics or biology provide important guidance for real-world projects, but it is with the applied fields of engineering and medicine that we build bridges and cure patients. Within economics, it is also important to delineate the use of scientific principles in policymaking, as this type of categorization helps us understand where progress has been made and where further progress is most needed. I will categorize the applied science of monetary policy as those aspects that involve systematic, or algorithmic, methods such as the development of econometric models. Other, more judgmental aspects of policymaking are what I will call the "art" of policymaking.

So, how have the basic scientific principles outlined above been used algorithmically? I focus particularly on the U.S. examples because they are the ones I am most familiar with given my experience as an American central banker, but similar developments have occurred elsewhere.

Early Keynesian econometric models of the macroeconomy did not give monetary policy a prominent role (e.g. Tinbergen 1939; Adelman and Adelman 1959; Klein 1968). In contrast, the policy-oriented models developed in the 1960s – such as the MIT-Penn-SSRC (MPS) model, developed by Franco Modigliani and collaborators and used as the workhorse model for policy analysis at the Federal Reserve until 1996 – incorporated a very important role for monetary policy, broadly similar to the main channels of the monetary policy transmission mechanism that are embedded in the current generation of models.[15]

In this sense, the notion that inflation is a monetary phenomenon has been embedded in formal models for several decades.

Very early versions of the MPS model did display a long-run trade-off between unemployment and inflation, as the principle that there should be no long-run trade-off took some time to be accepted (e.g. Gramlich 2004). By the early 1970s, the principle of no long-run trade-off was fully ensconced in the MPS model by the adoption of an accelerationist Phillips curve (Pierce and Enzler 1974; Brayton et al. 1997). The recognition in their models that lower unemployment could not be bought by accepting higher inflation was a factor driving central banks to adopt anti-inflationary policies by the 1980s.

Although accelerationist Phillips curves became standard in macroeconometric models used at central banks like the MPS model through the 1970s, expectational elements were still largely missing. The next generation of models emphasized the importance of expectations. For example, the staff at the Board of Governors of the Federal Reserve System developed their next-generation model, FRB/US (Brayton and Tinsley 1995; Reifschneider, Stockton, and Wilcox 1997; Reifschneider, Tetlow, and Williams 1999), to incorporate the importance of expectations in the determination of real activity and inflation. The FRB/US model, and similar models developed at other central banks such as the Bank of Canada's QPM model (Coletti et al. 1996) and the Reserve Bank of New Zealand's FPS model (Hunt, Rose, and

Scott 2000) were an outgrowth of the rational expectations revolution, and they allowed expectations to be derived under many different assumptions, including rational expectations. Policy simulations to help guide monetary policy decisions, such as those that are shown to the Federal Open Market Committee (FOMC), explicitly emphasize assumptions about future expectations and how they are formed. Policymakers have thus come to recognize that their decisions about policy involve not only the current policy setting but also how they may be thinking about future policy settings.

The focus on optimizing economic agents coming out of the rational expectations revolution has led to modeling efforts at central banks that not only make use of rational expectations, but that are also grounded on sounder microfoundations. Specifically, these models build on two recent literatures, real business cycle theory (e.g. Prescott 1986) and New-Keynesian theory (e.g. Mankiw and Romer 1991). In contrast to older Keynesian macro modeling, New-Keynesian theory provides microfoundations for Keynesian concepts such as nominal rigidities, the non-neutrality of money, and the inefficiency of business cycle fluctuations by deriving them from optimizing behavior. The real business cycle approach makes use of stochastic general equilibrium growth models with representative, optimizing agents. The resulting new class of models, in which New-Keynesian features such as nominal rigidities and monopolistic competition are added to the frictionless real business models, have become known as dynamic stochastic general equilibrium (DSGE) models. Simple versions of such models have already provided a framework in which to think about key aspects of monetary policy design – insights perhaps best illustrated in the Woodford (2003) discussion of policy issues in the now-textbook, three-equation New-Keynesian model. Larger,

---

[15] Brayton and Mauskopf (1985) describe the MPS model. As pointed out by Gramlich (2004), the researchers at the Federal Reserve were instrumental in the building of this model and it might more accurately be described as the Fed-MIT model or the Fed-MIT-Penn model.

more empirically-motivated DSGE models are now in their early stages of development and are beginning to be used for policy analysis at central banks (e.g. at the European Central Bank, Smets and Wouters 2003, and Coenen, McAdam, and Straub 2007; and at the Federal Reserve Board, Erceg, Guerrieri, and Gust 2006, and Edge, Kiley, and Laforte 2007).

There are two very important implications from policy analysis with DSGE models, as emphasized by Galí and Gertler (2007): First, "monetary transmission depends critically on private sector expectations of the future path of the central bank's policy instrument." Second, "the natural (flexible price equilibrium) values of both output and the real interest rate provide important reference points for monetary policy – and may fluctuate considerably." I can attest that both of these propositions indeed are now featured in the Bluebook (the staff's main document for analyzing policy options for the FOMC).

The basic logic of the Taylor principle – that is, raising nominal interest rates more than one-for-one in response to an increase in inflation – was developed in conjunction with the analysis of Taylor's multicountry model and other macroeconometric models (Taylor 1993a, b; Bryant, Hooper, and Mann 1993). However, although the Taylor principle is a necessary condition for good monetary policy outcomes, it is not sufficient. Central bankers require knowledge about how much difference the Taylor principle makes to monetary policy outcomes. They also require an understanding of how much greater than one the response of nominal interest rates should be to increases in inflation and also need to know how the policy rate should respond to other variables. Studying the performance of different rules in macroeconometric models has become a major enterprise at central banks, and the conclusion is that the Taylor principle is indeed very important. Analysis of policy rules in

macroeconometric models that are not fully based on optimizing agents has been very extensive (e.g. Bryant, Hooper, and Mann 1993; Levin, Wieland, and Williams 1999), and we are now seeing similar analysis using DSGE models (e.g. Levin et al. 2006; Schmitt-Grohé and Uribe 2006).

The second principle, and the sixth through the eighth principles – which emphasize the benefits of price stability and the importance of the time-inconsistency problem, central bank independence and a commitment to a nominal anchor – have important applications to the design of monetary policy institutions.

The argument that independent central banks perform better and are better able to resist the pressures for overly expansionary monetary policy arising from the time-inconsistency problem has led to a remarkable trend toward increasing central bank independence. Before the 1990s, only a few central banks were highly independent, most notably the Bundesbank, the Swiss National Bank, and, to a somewhat lesser extent, the Federal Reserve. Now almost all central banks in advanced countries and many in emerging-market countries have central banks with a level of independence on par with or exceeding that of the Federal Reserve. In the 1990s, greater independence was granted to central banks in such diverse countries as Japan, New Zealand, South Korea, Sweden, the United Kingdom, and those in the euro zone.

The increasing recognition of the time-inconsistency problem and the role of a nominal anchor in producing better economic outcomes has been an important impetus behind increasing central banks' commitments to nominal anchors. One resulting dramatic development in recent years has been a new monetary policy strategy, inflation targeting – the public announcement of medium-term numerical targets for inflation with commitment and accountability to achieve this target, along with increased transparency of the monetary policy strategy through communication with the public (Bernanke and Mishkin 1997). There has been a remarkable trend toward inflation targeting, which was adopted first by New Zealand in March 1990, and has since been adopted by an additional 23 countries (Rose 2006). The evidence, is in general quite favorable to inflation targeting, although countries that have adopted inflation targeting have not improved their monetary policy performance beyond that of nontargeters in industrial countries that have had successful monetary policy (e.g. Bernanke et al. 1999; Mishkin and Schmidt-Hebbel 2002, 2007; Rose 2006). And, in contrast to other monetary policy regimes, no country with its own currency that has adopted inflation targeting has been forced to abandon it.[16]

The scientific principle that financial frictions matter to economic fluctuations has led to increased attention at central banks to concerns about financial stability. Many central banks now publish so-called Financial Stability reports, which examine vulnerabilities to the financial system that could have negative consequences for economic activity in the future. Other central banks are involved in prudential regulation and supervision of the financial system to reduce excessive risk-taking that could lead to financial instability. Central banks also have designed their lending facilities to improve their ability to function as a lender of last resort, so they can provide liquidity quickly to the financial system in case of financial disruptions.

## The Art of Monetary Policy

I have argued that there have been major advances in the science of monetary policy in recent years, both in terms of basic scientific principles and applications of these principles

to the real world of monetary policymaking. Monetary policy has indeed become more of a science. There are, however, serious limitations to the science of monetary policy. Thus, as former vice-chairman of the Federal Reserve Board, Alan Blinder (1998, p.17), has emphasized, "central banking in practice is as much art as science." By "art," I mean the use of judgment – judgment that is informed by economic theory and data but in a manner that is less explicitly tied to formal models or algorithms.

There are several reasons why judgment will always be an important element in the conduct of monetary policy. First, models are able to make use of only a small fraction of the potentially valuable information that tells us about the complexity of the economy. For example, there are very high frequency data – monthly, weekly, and daily – that are not incorporated into macroeconometric models, which are usually estimated on quarterly data. These high-frequency data can often be very informative about the near-term dynamics of the economy and are used judgmentally by central-bank forecasters (e.g. Reifschneider, Stockton, and Wilcox 1997).

Second, information that can be very useful in forecasting the economy or deciding whether a particular model makes sense is often anecdotal and is thus not easily quantifiable. The Federal Reserve makes extensive use of anecdotal information in producing its forecasts. The staff at the Board and the Federal Reserve Banks monitor a huge amount of anecdotal information, and such information is discussed extensively in the publicly released Beige Book, which reports information from contacts in the Federal Reserve Districts, and by the participants in FOMC meetings.

---

[16] Spain and Finland gave up inflation targeting when they entered the euro zone.

Third, although monetary policymakers make extensive use of models in both forecasting and evaluating different policies, they are never sure that one model is the correct one. Active, and sometimes bitter, debates about which modeling approaches are the right ones are ongoing in macroeconomics, and there often is not a consensus on the best model. As a result, central banks must express some degree of humility regarding their knowledge of the structural relationships that determine activity and prices. This humility is readily apparent in the practice at central banks, which involves looking at many different models – structural, reduced-form, general equilibrium and partial equilibrium, and continually using judgment to decide which models are most informative.

Fourth, the economy does not stand still but, rather, changes over time. Economic relationships are thus unlikely to remain stable, and it is not always clear how these relationships are changing.[17] Therefore, policymakers must sometimes put less weight on econometrically estimated equations and instead make informed guesses about how the economy will evolve.

Fifth, as part of managing expectations, monetary policymakers communicate with economic agents who are not automatons but instead process information in complex ways. Subtle changes can make a big difference in the effectiveness of communication strategies – i.e., details matter – and judgment is therefore always an important element of good communication.[18]

Although, for the reasons outlined above, judgment will always be a necessary element of monetary policy, good decisions require that judgment be disciplined – not too ad hoc – and be well informed by the science of monetary policy. As Blinder (1998, p. 17), has put it, "Nonetheless, while practicing this dark art, I have always found the science quite useful." Here I will discuss two recent episodes in the United States – the financial-headwinds period in the early 1990s and the new-economy, productivity burst of the late 1990s – to illustrate how judgment informed by science was able to produce good economic outcomes.

## Financial Headwinds in the Early 1990s

The last scientific principle discussed in the chapter's first section emphasizes the link between financial frictions and the business cycle, but it is unfortunately quite hard to model the role of these frictions in a general equilibrium, macroeconometric model. The late 1980s saw a boom and then a major bust in the commercial real estate market leading to huge loan losses that caused a substantial fall in capital at depository institutions (banks). At the same time, regulators were raising bank capital requirements to ensure compliance with the regulatory framework, known as Basel Accord. The resulting capital shortfalls meant that banks had to either raise new capital or restrict their asset growth by cutting back on lending. Because of their weak condition, banks could not raise much new capital, so they chose the latter course. The resulting slowdown in the growth of credit was unprecedented in the post-world war-two era (Reifschneider, Stockton, and Wilcox 1997). Because banks have informational advantages in making certain loans (e.g. Mishkin 2007a), many bank-dependent borrowers could no longer get access to financing and thus had to cut back on their spending.

---

[17] The housing channel is one example in which the monetary transmission mechanism has changed substantially and is likely to continue to do so over time, e.g. Bernanke (2007) and Mishkin (2007c).

[18] Because subtle details matter, there is an important rationale for the use of case studies to research best practice in central bank communication strategies and this is why I have been drawn to case-study research (Bernanke and Mishkin 1992; Bernanke et al. 1999; Mishkin 1999).

Although the large-scale macromodel then in use at the Federal Reserve Board did not explicitly have financial frictions in its equations, officials at the Federal Reserve were aware that these frictions could be very important and were concerned that they might be playing a critical role at that juncture. In part reflecting this concern, many Fed economists were actively engaged in research on the impact of bank credit on economic activity. This research, together with anecdotal reports that businesses were finding themselves credit constrained and survey information indicating that bank credit standards were being tightened, gave rise to the view among Federal Reserve policymakers that the capital crunch at banks was noticeably constraining credit flows and hence spending by households and firms. Indeed, Federal Reserve Chairman Alan Greenspan (1992) suggested that financial conditions in the early-1990s was holding back activity like a "50-mile per hour headwind," and in that period the FOMC reduced the Federal Funds Rate to levels well below that suggested by the Taylor rule (e.g. Rudebusch 2006). Indeed, the recovery from the 1990-91 recession was very slow, and the Fed kept the Federal Funds Rate at 3 percent (which, with an inflation rate of around 3 percent, implied a real rate of zero) until February of 1994 – a very accommodative policy stance. The Fed's expansionary policy stance at the time has in hindsight been judged as very successful, with the economy finally recovering and inflation remaining contained.

## The New-Economy, Productivity Burst of the Late 1990s

By the beginning of 1997, the unemployment rate had declined to 5.3 percent, and the Board staff was forecasting that the unemployment rate would fall to 5 percent – an outcome that followed by midyear. The forecast of a 5 percent unemployment rate was well below most estimates of the NAIRU (nonaccelerating

inflation rate of unemployment). As a result, the staff forecast was for a rise in inflation (Svensson and Tetlow 2005). The staff forecast and the recommendation in the February Bluebook suggested that a period of monetary policy tightening would be needed to "forestall a continuous rise in core inflation" (Federal Reserve Board 1997, p. 7). Although the FOMC did raise the Federal Funds Rate in March 1997, it desisted from raising rates further; in fact, the FOMC reduced the Federal Funds Rate in the fall of 1998 after the episode involving the Long-Term Capital Management hedge fund and the Russian-bond meltdown. Despite an unemployment rate continually below estimates of the NAIRU, the outcome was not the acceleration that the Board staff's models predicted (Svensson and Tetlow 2005; Tetlow and Ironside 2006) but instead a decline in the inflation rate.

Why did the FOMC hold off and not raise rates in the face of economic growth that was forecasted to be far in excess of potential growth – a decision that, ex post, appears to have resulted in desirable outcomes for inflation and employment? The answer is that Fed Chairman Greenspan guessed correctly that something unusual was going on with productivity. For example, he was hearing from businesspeople that new information technologies were transforming their businesses, making it easier for them to raise productivity. He was also a big fan of the historical work by Paul David (1990), which suggested that new technological innovations often took years to produce accelerations in productivity in the overall economy (Meyer 2004). Greenspan was led to the conclusion that the trend in productivity growth was accelerating, a conclusion that the Board staff's forecast did not come to fully accept until late 1999 (Svensson and Tetlow 2005). Moreover, he appeared to be convinced that the acceleration in productivity would cap inflationary pressures, implying that inflation would not accelerate even with rapid economic growth. His view prevailed in the FOMC (Meyer 2004).[19]

The types of information used to foresee the effects of a productivity acceleration are inherently difficult to incorporate into formal models. This is obvious with respect to the anecdotes I have mentioned. But even the systematic data available at the time required the use of judgment. For example, part of the story of the late 1990s reflected the different signals being sent by real-time measures of gross domestic product and gross domestic income – or at least the component of the latter produced by nonfinancial corporations, which is perhaps better measured (Corrado and Slifman 1999) and provided some advance signal of the productivity acceleration. Of course, these two measures – GDP and GDI – are the same in our formal models, and only a judgmental filtering of the information content in each can be useful in real time.

Good judgment benefits not only from a good feel for the data and the successful processing of anecdotal information but also from the use of scientific models, and the late-1990s episode is no exception. At the July 1997 FOMC meeting, the Board staff presented simulations using the FRB/US model examining what would happen if productivity were to accelerate (Meyer 2004; Tetlow and Ironside 2006). Their simulations produced several results that were consistent with what seemed to be happening. An acceleration of productivity would raise profits and the value of equities, which would boost aggregate demand because higher stock values would stimulate business investment and boost consumer spending through wealth effects. The acceleration in productivity would also be disinflationary and could therefore explain why inflation would fall despite a declining unemployment rate. An unexpected rise in productivity growth would not be immediately reflected in higher wage rates, so unit labor costs (wages adjusted for productivity growth) would fall, leading to a decline in inflation. Another way of looking at this is through the NAIRU framework. For a given rate of unemployment, an unexpected acceleration in productivity would produce an inflation rate lower than it otherwise would be, so that the NAIRU at which the unemployment rate would not lead to an acceleration of inflation would decline. As events unfolded in line with these simulation results, the FOMC became more convinced that a productivity boom was under way and that there was less need for a monetary tightening.

The two episodes discussed here illustrate several points about the art of central banking. First, monetary policy is more likely to produce better outcomes when central bankers recognize the limitations of their formal models. However, judgment cannot be undisciplined. The accuracy of judgment is likely to be enhanced when it is informed by the science of monetary policy, either through use of model simulations or applications of basic scientific principles.

## Further Advances to Make Monetary Policy More of a Science

Although art will always be a feature of monetary policy, the science of monetary policy will keep advancing, making monetary policy more of a science. In this section I will briefly discuss where I think future advances in the science of monetary policy are likely to be made.

The push to build sound microfoundations into general equilibrium macroeconometric models is ongoing as the expanding literature on DSGE models indicates (see the survey in Galí and Gertler 2007; and the discussions of model

---

[19] Greenspan's successful use of judgment during this period is one reason why he was dubbed the "maestro" by Woodward (2000).

enhancements in Erceg, Gust, and Guerrieri 2006, and in Edge, Kiley, and Laforte 2007). However, these DSGE models are only now starting to be brought to the data and are not nearly as rich in their coverage of features of the economy as are older, more-Keynesian models such as FRB/US.[20] Models like FRB/US do have elements that are more ad hoc, but at the current juncture central bankers see them as more realistic. Building macroeconometric models thoroughly grounded on solid microfoundations, but with treatment of more sectors of the economy, will be one of the main challenges for the science of monetary policy in the future.

Nominal rigidities are central to understanding quantitatively the impact of monetary policy on the economy. The canonical DSGE model makes use of a simple New-Keynesian Phillips curve framework because it makes the model very tractable.[21] This framework is highly stylized, however, and does not allow for endogenous changes in how often contracts are renegotiated. Furthermore, there may be other reasons why prices are not reset too often, such as rational inattention.[22] Better explanations – and more empirical validation – regarding the source of nominal rigidities may lead to important advances in the science of monetary policy.[23]

Tractability has led to models based on microfoundations, such as DSGE models, to rely on representative agents, which is a serious drawback. I have a strong sense that what drives many macroeconomic phenomena that are particularly interesting is heterogeneity of economic agents. Building heterogeneous agents into macroeconometric models will

by no means be easy, but it has the potential to make these models much more realistic. Furthermore, it may allow us to understand the link between aggregate economic fluctuations and income distribution, a hot topic in political circles. Heterogeneity of economic agents is also crucial to understanding labor market frictions. In some DSGE models, all fluctuations in employment are from variation in hours per worker, and yet in the real world, changes in unemployment are a more important source of employment fluctuations. Bringing the search and matching literature more directly into microfounded macroeconometric models will make them more realistic and also allow better welfare comparisons of different monetary policies.

Although, as discussed above, monetary policymakers understand the importance of financial frictions to the business cycle, general equilibrium macroeconometric models, for the most part, ignore financial market imperfections. Research has begun to incorporate financial market imperfections into quantitative dynamic general equilibrium models (e.g. Bernanke, Gertler, and Gilchrist 1999), and some of this research has even begun to estimate these types of DSGE models (e.g. Christiano, Motto, and Rostagno 2007). But we need to know a lot more about the how to scientifically incorporate financial frictions into policy deliberations. For the time being, the role for art is this area is very important.

The new field of behavioral economics, which makes use of concepts from other social sciences such as anthropology, sociology, and, particularly, psychology, suggests that economic agents may not always be the rational, optimizing

---

[20] To be fair, models like FRB/US do have much in common with DSGE models in that many of their equations, but not all, are built on solid microfoundations.

[21] These models often use the Calvo (1983) staggering construct or the quadratic adjustment costs of Rotemberg (1982); these specifications yield identical Phillips curve specifications.

[22] Mankiw and Reis (2002) introduce this type of model; Kiley (2007) compares the ability of this type of model to improve upon the fit of more familiar sticky-price models.

[23] Microeconomic studies have begun to make interesting progress (e.g. Bils and Klenow 2004; Nakamura and Steinsson 2006).

agents we assume in our models. Embedding behavioral economics into macro models can make a major difference in the way these models work (Akerlof 2007). How important are deviations from rationality to our views on the monetary transmission mechanism, and what are welfare-enhancing monetary policies? How can systematic deviations from rationality be modeled in a serious way and built into macroeconometric models? Answers to these questions may further enhance the realism of macroeconometric models used for policy purposes.

One of the rationales for the use of judgment (art) in the conduct of monetary policy is that the economy is not stationary, but rather is changing all the time. This means that economic agents are continually learning about the state of the economy, so the rational expectations assumption that depends on stationarity to derive expectations often may not be valid. Research on the how agents learn and its implications for business cycles is an active area of research (Bullard and Mitra 2002; Evans and Honkapohja 2003) that should have major payoff in helping us to better understand the impact of monetary policy on the economy.

Another rationale for keeping art in monetary policymaking is that we can never be sure what is the right model of the economy. As I mentioned earlier, this argues for humility at central banks. It also argues for advances in scientific techniques to think about which monetary policies are more robust in producing good economic outcomes. Research in this area is also very active. One approach examines parametric uncertainties in which methods are examined to ensure that a prescribed policy works well in an entire class of models (e.g. Levin, Wieland, and Williams 1999). Nonparametric approaches look at designing policies that protect against model misspecifications that cannot be measured (e.g. Hansen and Sargent 2007; Tetlow and von zur Muehlen 2001).

The list of areas here that will advance the science of monetary policy is necessarily incomplete. Some of the most important advances in economic science are often very hard to predict.

## Concluding Remarks

The science of monetary policy has come a long way over the past fifty years, and I would argue that its advances are an important reason for the policy successes that so many countries have been experiencing in recent years. Monetary policy will however never become as boring as dentistry. Monetary policy will always have elements of art as well as science. However, the advances in the science of monetary policy that I have described here suggest that monetary policy will become more of a science over time. Furthermore, even though art will always be a key element in the conduct of monetary policy, the more it is informed by good science, the more successful monetary policy will be.

## REFERENCES

Adelman, I., and F. L. Adelman. 1959. "The Dynamic Properties of the Klein-Goldberger Model." *Econometrica*, 27: 596-625.

Akerlof, G. A. 1970. "The Market for 'Lemons': Quality, Uncertainty and the Market Mechanism." *Quarterly Journal of Economics*, 84: 488-500.

Akerlof, G. A. 2007. "The Missing Motivation in Macroeconomics." *American Economic Review*, 97: 5-36.

Akerlof, G. A., W. R. Dickens, and G. L. Perry. 1996. "The Macroeconomics of Low Inflation." *Brookings Papers on Economic Activity*, 1996: 1-59.

Alesina, A., and L. H. Summers. 1993. "Central Bank Independence and Macroeconomic Performance: Some Comparative Evidence." *Journal of Money, Credit and Banking*, 25: 151-62.

Anderson, P., and D. Gruen. 1995. "Macroeconomic Policies and Growth." In *Productivity and Growth: Proceedings of a Conference held at the H.C. Coombs Centre for Financial Studies, Kirribilli*, ed. P. Anderson, J. Dwyer and D. Gruen, 279-319. Sydney : Reserve Bank of Australia, Economic Group.

Barro, R. J. 1977. "Unanticipated Money Growth and Unemployment in the United States." *American Economic Review*, 67: 101-15.

Barro, R. J., and D. B. Gordon. 1983. "Rules, Discretion, and Reputation in a Model of Monetary Policy." *Journal of Monetary Economics*, 12: 101-22.

Bernanke, B. S. 1983. "Nonmonetary Effects of the Financial Crisis in the Propagation of the Great Depression." *American Economic Review*, 73: 257-76.

Bernanke, B. S. 2007. "Housing, Housing Finance, and Monetary Policy." Speech delivered at the Federal Reserve Bank of Kansas City's Economic Symposium, Jackson Hole, WY, August 31.

Bernanke, B. S., and M. Gertler. 1999. "Monetary Policy and Asset Price Volatility." In *New Challenges for Monetary Policy*, Federal Reserve Bank of Kansas City, 77-128. Kansas City: Federal Reserve Bank of Kansas City.

Bernanke, B. S., and M. Gertler. 2001. "Should Central Banks Respond to Movements in Asset Prices?", *American Economic Review*, 91(2): 253-57.

Bernanke, B. S., M. Gertler, and S. Gilchrist. 1999. "The Financial Accelerator in a Quantitative Business Cycle Framework." In *Handbook of Macroeconomics*, 1, part 3, ed. J. B. Taylor and M. Woodford, 1341-93. Amsterdam: North-Holland.

Bernanke, B., and F. Mishkin. 1992. "Central Bank Behavior and the Strategy of Monetary Policy: Observations from Six Industrialized Countries." In *NBER Macroeconomics Annual 1992*, Volume 7, 183-228. Cambrige, MA: MIT Press.

Bernanke, B. S., and F. S. Mishkin. 1997. "Inflation Targeting: A New Framework for Monetary Policy?" *Journal of Economic Perspectives*, 11: 97-116.

Bernanke, B. S., T. Laubach, F. S. Mishkin, and A. S. Posen. 1999. *Inflation Targeting: Lessons from the International Experience*. Princeton, NJ: Princeton University Press.

Bils, M., and P. J. Klenow. 2004. "Some Evidence on the Importance of Sticky Prices." *Journal of Political Economics*, 112: 947-85.

Blinder, A. S. 1998. *Central Banking in Theory and Practice*. Cambridge, MA: MIT Press.

Brayton, F., A. Levin, R. Lyon, and J. C. Williams. 1997. "The Evolution of Macro Models at the Federal Reserve Board." *Carnegie-Rochester Conference Series on Public Policy*, 47: 43-81.

Brayton, F., and P. Tinsley. 1996. "A Guide to FRB/US: A New Macroeconomic Model of the United States." Finance and Economics Discussion Series, 1996-42. Washington: Board of Governors of the Federal Reserve System.

Brayton, F., and E. Mauskopf. 1985. "The Federal Reserve Board MPS Quarterly Econometric Model of the U.S. Economy." *Economic Modelling*, 2(3): 170-292.

Briault, C. 1995. "The Costs of Inflation." Bank of England Quarterly Bulletin, 35: 33-45.

Bryant, R. C., P. Hooper, and C. L. Mann. 1993. *Evaluating Policy Regimes: New Research in Empirical Macroeconomics*. Washington: Brookings Institution.

Bullard, J., and K. Mitra. 2002. "Learning about Monetary Policy Rules." *Journal of Monetary Economics*, 49: 1105-29.

Calomiris, C. W. 1993. "Financial Factors in the Great Depression." *Journal of Economic Perspectives*, 7: 61-85.

Calvo, G. A. 1978. "On the Time Consistency of Optimal Policy in a Monetary Economy." *Econometrica*, 46: 1411-28.

Calvo, G. A. 1983. "Staggered Prices in a Utility-Maximizing Framework." *Journal of Monetary Economics*, 12(3): 383-398.

Christiano, L., R. Motto, and M. Rostagno. 2007. "Shocks, Structures or Monetary Policies? The EA and US After 2001." European Central Bank Working Paper Series 774.

Clarida, R., J. Galí, and M. Gertler. 1998. "Monetary Policy Rules and Macroeconomic Stability: Evidence and Some Theory." *Quarterly Journal of Economics*, 115: 147-80.

Clarida, R., J. Galí, and M. Gertler. 1999. "The Science of Monetary Policy: A New Keynesian Perspective." *Journal of Economic Literature*, 37: 1661-1707.

Coenen, G., P. McAdam, and R. Straub. 2007. "Tax Reform and Labour Market Performance in the Euro Area: A Simulation-Based Analysis Using the New Area-Wide Model." European Central Bank Working Paper Series 747.

Coletti, D., B. Hunt, D. Rose, and R. Tetlow. 1996. "The Bank of Canada's New Quarterly Projection Model. Part 3 , the Dynamic Model : QPM." Bank of Canada Technical Reports 75.

Corrado, C., and L. Slifman. 1999. "Decomposition of Productivity and Unit Costs." *American Economic Review*, 89: 328-32.

Cukierman, A. 1993. "Central Bank Independence, Political Influence and Macroeconomic Performance: A Survey of Recent Developments." *Cuadernos de Economía*, 30: 271-91.

Cukierman, A. 2006. "Central Bank Independence and Monetary Policy Making Institutions: Past, Present, and Future." *Journal Economía Chilena*, 9: 5-23.

David, P. A. 1990. "The Dynamo and the Computer: An Historical Perspective on the Modern Productivity Paradox." *American Economic Review*, 80: 355-61.

Edge, R. M., M. T. Kiley, and J.-P. Laforte. 2007. "Natural Rate Measures in an Estimated DSGE Model of the U.S. Economy." Finance and Economics Discussion Series, 2007-8, Washington, Board of Governors of the Federal Reserve System.

Eggertsson, G. B., and M. Woodford. 2003. "The Zero Bound on Interest Rates and Optimal Monetary Policy." *Brookings Papers on Economic Activity*, 2003, 139-211.

English, W. B. 1996. "Inflation and Financial Sector Size." Finance and Economics Discussion Series, 1996-16, Washington, Board of Governors of the Federal Reserve System.

Erceg, C., L. Guerrieri, and C. Gust. 2006. "SIGMA: A New Open Economy Model for Policy Analysis." *International Journal of Central Banking*, 2: 1-50.

Evans, G. W., and S. Honkapohja. 2003. "Adaptive Learning and Monetary Policy Design." *Journal of Money, Credit and Banking*, 35: 1045-72.

Fatás, A., I. Mihov, and A. K. Rose. 2007. "Quantitative Goals for Monetary Policy." *Journal of Money, Credit and Banking*, 39: 1163-76.

Federal Reserve Board. 1997. *Monetary Policy Alternatives*. Washington: Board of Governors of the Federal Reserve System.

Feldstein, M. 1997. "The Costs and Benefits of Going from Low Inflation to Price Stability." In *Reducing Inflation: Motivation and Strategy*, ed. C. D. Romer and D. H. Romer, 123-66. Chicago: University of Chicago Press.

Fischer, S. 1993. "The Role of Macroeconomic Factors in Growth." *Journal of Monetary Economics*, 32: 485-512.

Fischer, S. 1994. "Modern Central Banking." In *The Future of Central Banking: The Tercentenary Symposium of the Bank of England*, ed. F. Capie et al. Cambridge, U.K.: Cambridge University Press.

Fischer, S., and G. Debelle. 1994. "How Independent Should a Central Bank Be?" In *Goals, Guidelines, and Constraints Facing Monetary Policymakers, Proceedings from the Federal Reserve Bank of Boston Conference Series* No. 38, 195-221. Boston: Federal Reserve Bank of Boston.

Fisher, I. 1933. "The Debt-Deflation Theory of Great Depressions." *Econometrica*, 1: 337-57.

Forder, J. 2000. "Traps in the Measurement of Independence and Accountability of Central Banks." University of Oxford Economics Series Working Papers 023.

Friedman, M. 1963. Inflation: *Causes and Consequences*. New York: Asia Publishing House.

Friedman, M. 1968. "The Role of Monetary Policy." *American Economic Review*, 58: 1-17.

Friedman, M., and D. Meiselman. 1963. "The Relative Stability of Monetary Velocity and the Investment Multiplier in the United States, 1897-1958." In *Stabilization Policies, a Series of Research Studies Prepared for the Commission on Money and Credit*, 165-268. Englewood Cliffs, NJ: Prentice-Hall.

Friedman, M., and A. J. Schwartz. 1963a. "Monetary History of the United States, 1867-1960." National Bureau of Economic Research Publications, Princeton, NJ: Princeton University Press.

Friedman, M., and A. J. Schwartz. 1963b. "Money and Business Cycles." *Review of Economics and Statistics*, 45: 32-64.

Galí, J., and M. Gertler. 2007. "Macroeconomic Modeling for Monetary Policy Evaluation." *Journal of Economic Perspectives*, 21: 25-46.

Goodfriend, M. 1993. "Interest Rate Policy and the Inflation Scare Problem: 1979-1992." Federal Reserve Bank of Richmond, Economic Quarterly, 79: 1-24.

Goodfriend, M. and R. King. 1997. "The New Neoclassical Synthesis and the Role of Monetary Policy." In *NBER macroeconomics annual 1997*, ed. B. S. Bernanke and J. J. Rotemberg, 231-83. Cambridge, MA: MIT Press.

Gramlich, E. M. 2005. "The Board's Modeling Work in the 1960s." In *Models and Monetary Policy: Research in the Tradition of Dale Henderson, Richard Porter, and Peter Tinsley*. Washington: Board of Governors of the Federal Reserve System.

Greenspan, A. 1992. "Testimony before the Committee on Banking, Housing, and Urban Affairs." U.S. Senate, July 21.

Greenwald, B., J. E. Stiglitz, and A. Weiss. 1984. "Informational Imperfections in the Capital Market and Macroeconomic Fluctuations." *American Economic Review*, 74: 194-99

Hansen, L. P., and T. J. Sargent. 2007. *Robustness*. Princeton, NJ: Princeton University Press.

Hunt, B., D. Rose, and A. Scott. 2000. "The Core Model of the Reserve Bank of New Zealand's Forecasting and Policy System." *Economic Modelling*, 172: 247-74.

Kashyap, A. K., and J. C. Stein. 1994. "Monetary Policy and Bank Lending." In *Monetary Policy*, ed. N. G. Mankiw, National Bureau of Economic Research, Studies in Business Cycles, 29, 221-56. Chicago: University of Chicago Press.

Kiley, M. T. 2007. "A Quantitative Comparison of Sticky-Price and Sticky-Information Models of Price Setting." *Journal of Money, Credit and Banking*, 39(s1), 101-25.

Klein, L. R. 1968. *An Essay on the Theory of Economic Prediction*. Helsinki: Yrjö Jahnssonin Säätiö.

Kydland, F. E., and E. C. Prescott. 1977. "Rules Rather Than Discretion: The Inconsistency of Optimal Plans." *Journal of Political Economy*, 85: 473-92.

Levin, A., V. Wieland, and J. C. Williams. 1999. "Robustness of Simple Monetary Policy Rules under Model Uncertainty." In *Monetary Policy Rules*, ed. J. B. Taylor, National Bureau of Economic Research, Studies in Business Cycles, 31, 263-99. Chicago: University of Chicago Press.

Levin, A. T., A. Onatski, J. Williams, and N. M. Williams. 2005. "Monetary Policy Under Uncertainty in Micro-Founded Macroeconometric Models." In *NBER Macroeconomics Annual 2005*, ed. M. Gertler and K. Rogoff, 229-87. Cambridge, MA: MIT Press.

Lucas, R. E. 1972. "Expectations and the Neutrality of Money." *Journal of Economic Theory*, 4: 103-24.

Lucas, R. E. 1973. "Some International Evidence on Output-Inflation Tradeoffs." *American Economic Review*, 63: 326-34.

Lucas, R., Jr. 1976. "Econometric Policy Evaluation: A Critique." *Carnegie-Rochester Conference Series on Public Policy*, 1(1): 19-46.

Mankiw, N. G., and R. Reis. 2002. "Sticky Information Versus Sticky Prices: A Proposal to Replace the New Keynesian Phillips Curve." *Quarterly Journal of Economics*, 117: 1295-1328.

Mankiw, N. G., and D. Romer. 1991. *New Keynesian Economics*. Cambridge, MA: MIT Press.

Meyer, L. H. 2004. *A Term at the Fed: An Insider's View*. New York: Harper Business.

Mishkin, F. S. 1978. "The Household Balance Sheet and the Great Depression." *Journal of Economic History*, 38: 918-37.

Mishkin, F. S. 1981. "The Real Interest Rate: An Empirical Investigation." *Carnegie-Rochester Conference Series on Public Policy*, 15: 151-200.

Mishkin, F. S. 1982a. "Does Anticipated Monetary Policy Matter? An Econometric Investigation." *Journal of Political Economy*, 90: 22-51.

Mishkin, F. S. 1982b. "Does Anticipated Aggregate Demand Policy Matter? Further Econometric Results." *American Economic Review*, 72: 788-802.

Mishkin, F. S. 1983. *A Rational Expectations Approach to Macroeconometrics: Testing Policy Ineffectiveness and Efficient Markets Models*. Chicago: University of Chicago Press.

Mishkin, F. S. 1991. "Asymmetric Information and Financial Crises: A Historical Perspective." In *Financial Markets and Financial Crises*, ed. R. G. Hubbard, 69-108. Chicago: University of Chicago Press.

Mishkin, F. S. 1992. "Is the Fisher Effect for Real? A Reexamination of the Relationship Between Inflation and Interest Rates." *Journal of Monetary Economics*, 30: 195-215.

Mishkin, F. S. 1996. "Understanding Financial Crises: A Developing Country Perspective." In *Annual World Bank Conference on Development Economics 1996*, ed. M. Bruno and B. Pleskovic, 29-62. Washington: World Bank.

Mishkin, F. S. 1997. "The Causes and Propagation of Financial Instability: Lessons for Policymakers." In *Maintaining Financial Stability in a Global Economy*, 55-96. Kansas City: Federal Reserve Bank of Kansas City.

Mishkin, F. S. 1999. "International Experiences with Different Monetary Policy Regimes." *Journal of Monetary Economics*, 43: 579-605.

Mishkin, F. S. 2007a. *The Economics of Money, Banking, and Financial Markets*. 8th ed. Boston: Addison-Wesley.

Mishkin, F. S. 2007b. "Monetary Policy and the Dual Mandate." Speech delivered at Bridgewater College, Bridgewater, VA., April 10.

Mishkin, F. S. 2007c. "Housing and the Monetary Transmission Mechanism." Finance and Economics Discussion Series, 2007-40, Washington, Board of Governors of the Federal Reserve System.

Mishkin, F. S., and A. S. Posen. 1997. "Inflation Targeting: Lessons from Four Countries, Federal Reserve Bank of New York." *Economic Policy Review*, 3: 9-110.

Mishkin, F. S., and K. Schmidt-Hebbel. 2002. "One Decade of Inflation Targeting in the World: What Do We Know and What Do We Need to Know?" In *Inflation Targeting: Design, Performance, Challenges*, ed. N. Loayza and R. Soto, 171-219. Santiago: Central Bank of Chile.

Mishkin, F. S., and K. Schmidt-Hebbel. 2007. "Does Inflation Targeting Matter?" In *Monetary Policy Under Inflation Targeting*, ed. F. S. Mishkin and K. Schmidt-Hebbel, 291-372. Santiago: Central Bank of Chile.

Mishkin, F. S., and N. Westelius. Forthcoming. "Inflation Band Targeting and Optimal Inflation Contracts." *Journal of Money, Credit and Banking*.

Muth, J. F. 1961. "Rational Expectations and the Theory of Price Movements." *Econometrica*, 29: 315-35.

Myers, S. C., and N. S. Majluf. 1984. "Corporate Financing and Investment Decisions When Firms Have Information that Investors Do Not Have." *Journal of Financial Economics*, 13: 187-221.

Nakamura, E., and J. Steinsson. 2006. "Five Facts About Prices: A Reevaluation of Menu Cost Models." Mimeo, Harvard University.

Orphanides, A. 2003. "The Quest for Prosperity Without Inflation." *Journal of Monetary Economics*, 50: 633-63.

Phelps, E. S. 1968. "Money-Wage Dynamics and Labor-Market Equilibrium." *Journal of Political Economy*, 76: 687-711.

Phillips, A.W. 1958. "The Relation Between Unemployment and the Rate of Change of Money Wage Rates in the United Kingdom, 1861-1957." *Economica*, 25: 283-99.

**Pierce, J. L., and J. J. Enzler.** 1974. "The Effects of External Inflationary Shocks." *Brookings Papers on Economic Activity*, 1974, 13-54.

**Prescott, E. C.** 1986. "Theory Ahead of Business-Cycle Measurement." *Carnegie-Rochester Conference Series on Public Policy*, 25: 11-44.

**Reifschneider, D. L., D. J. Stockton, and D. W. Wilcox.** 1997. "Econometric Models and the Monetary Policy Process." *Carnegie-Rochester Conference Series on Public Policy*, 47: 1-37.

**Reifschneider, D., R. Tetlow, and J. Williams.** 1999. "Aggregate Disturbances, Monetary Policy, and the Macroeconomy: The FRB/US Perspective." Federal Reserve Bulletin, 85: 1-19.

**Reifschneider, D., and J. C. Williams.** 2000. "Three Lessons for Monetary Policy in a Low-Inflation Era." *Journal of Money, Credit and Banking*, 32: 936-66.

**Rose, A. K.** 2006. "A Stable International Monetary System Emerges: Inflation Targeting is Bretton Woods, Reversed." National Bureau of Economic Research Working Paper 12711.

**Rotemberg, J. J.** 1982. "Sticky Prices in the United States." *Journal of Political Economy*, 90: 1187-1211.

**Rudebusch, G. D.** 2006. "Monetary Policy Inertia: Fact or Fiction?" *International Journal of Central Banking*, 2: 85-135.

**Samuelson, P. A., and R. M. Solow.** 1960. "Analytical Aspects of Anti-Inflation Policy." *American Economic Review*, 50: 177-94.

**Schmitt-Grohé, S., and M. Uribe.** 2006. "Optimal Fiscal and Monetary Policy in a Medium-Scale Macroeconomic Model." European Central Bank Working Paper Series 612.

**Smets, F., and R. Wouters.** 2003. "An Estimated Dynamic Stochastic General Equilibrium Model of the Euro Area." *Journal of the European Economic Association*, 1: 1123-75.

**Svensson, L. E. O., and R. J. Tetlow.** 2005. "Optimal Policy Projections." *International Journal of Central Banking*, 1: 177-207.

**Taylor, J. B.** 1993a. "Discretion versus Policy Rules in Practice." *Carnegie-Rochester Conference Series on Public Policy*, 39: 195-214.

**Taylor, J. B.** 1993b. *Macroeconomic Policy in a World Economy: From Econometric Design to Practical Operation.* New York: Norton Press.

**Taylor, J. B. (ed.)** 1999. *Monetary Policy Rules.* National Bureau of Economic Research, Studies in Business Cycles, 31. Chicago: University of Chicago Press.

**Tetlow, R. J., and B. Ironside.** 2006. "Real-Time Model Uncertainty in the United States: The Fed from 1996-2003." European Central Bank Working Paper Series 610.

**Tetlow, R. J., and P. von zur Muehlen.** 2001. "Robust Monetary Policy with Misspecified Models: Does Model Uncertainty Always Call for Attenuated Policy?" *Journal of Economic Dynamics and Control*, 25: 911-49.

**Tinbergen, J.** 1939. *Business Cycles in the United States of America: 1919-1932.* Geneva: League of Nations.

**Woodford, M.** 2001. "The Taylor Rule and Optimal Monetary Policy." *American Economic Review*, 91: 232-7.

**Woodford, M.** 2003. *Interest and Prices: Foundations of a Theory of Monetary Policy.* Princeton, NJ: Princeton University Press.

**Woodward, B.** 2000. *Maestro: Greenspan's Fed and the American Boom.* New York: Simon & Schuster.

# THE DEUTSCHE BANK PRIZE
# IN FINANCIAL ECONOMICS 2007:
# AWARD CEREMONY
# AND SCIENTIFIC SYMPOSIUM
# IN HONOR OF
# MICHAEL WOODFORD

Josef Ackermann

# THE AWARD OF
# THE DEUTSCHE BANK PRIZE 2007

**Josef Ackermann (Deutsche Bank AG)**

Professor Woodford,
dear Mrs. Sbordone,
Minister Weimar and Corts,
Ladies and Gentlemen,

It is a great honor to welcome you here today to the award ceremony of the Deutsche Bank Prize in Financial Economics 2007, and in particular, to have an opportunity to congratulate the prize-winner Professor Michael Woodford. As most of you know, this is the second time we are celebrating this prize here at Villa Sander, following the award to Professor Eugene Fama two years ago.

Before I start, I would first like to thank all those who have made this event possible, most notably Professor Volker Wieland from the University of Frankfurt and the Center for Financial Studies, who served as the chairman of this year's jury and will be addressing you shortly. I would also like to thank the members of the jury, who spent a considerable amount of time and effort on selecting the winner from among the many high quality recommendations that they received. It is indeed an impressive jury, consisting of outstanding academics and central bankers, as well as a journalist and Deutsche Bank's Chief Economist.

Since Volker Wieland and Frederic Mishkin will highlight Professor Woodford's contributions to the field of monetary and financial economics, I will not go into much detail about his work, but I do want to stress how important this area of research is for the financial markets and the global economy in general.

Low and stable inflation rates as well as credible monetary policies are crucial for well-functioning financial markets. Without the stable framework created by central banks, we would not have seen the tremendous development and international integration of the world's financial markets over the past decades. In reaction to this, new products have been developed and the sharing of risk has spread to a continually increasing number of actors, products and countries – requiring more sophisticated risk management as well. In this sense, we have been witnesses to a mutually reinforcing trend of greater monetary and financial stability, greater market integration, and greater product variety.

To be able to perform this function, it is, of course, important for us to understand the advances in monetary economics to which Professor Woodford has contributed so capably. Here, as in so many areas, new fields of inquiry arise all the time and old ones may require new answers. The market difficulties emanating from the U.S. subprime market pose challenges to both central and commercial banks. And, closer to Professor Woodford's area of research, we have to analyze why the global surge in broad money since early-2006 has not led to higher inflation. Therefore, it is essential that the discussion continues between academics, central bankers and the financial sector. And – I would like to add – it is important to Deutsche Bank that Frankfurt should be one of the major financial centers where this discussion takes place. This afternoon's symposium on "The Theory and Practice of Monetary Policy Today"

at the University of Frankfurt was an important contribution in this regard. At Deutsche Bank, we are proud to have provided our support to this event.

But, ladies and gentlemen, our commitment does not end there. The Deutsche Bank Prize in Financial Economics is part of our contribution to the initiative "Finanzplatz Frankfurt" in order to support research and teaching in financial economics at the "House of Finance" of the University of Frankfurt and Goethe Business School.

This strong commitment to Frankfurt is only one part of our support for international research and reflects our belief that globalized financial markets need a worldwide network of international research and teaching with close ties to the major financial centers.

Furthermore, we believe it is important to bring top-notch research into alignment with market practices at the international level: Research and knowledge in financial economics and best practices from around the world must be discussed openly among professors and bankers, as well as politicians, regulators and central bankers. In light of the close interrelations in the world's capital markets, isolated discussions are inadequate. What we need is an ongoing dialogue at all levels.

To initiate our contribution to these discussions, we were pleased to award the first Deutsche Bank Prize in Financial Economics to Professor Eugene Fama in 2005 – and we are delighted about the selection of this year's laureate: Professor Michael Woodford!

Ladies and Gentlemen,

Well beyond the first Deutsche Bank Prize award ceremony itself, there was an unexpected impact on the general awareness of economic research in Germany: One of the most influential German newspapers, the *Frankfurter*

*Allgemeine Zeitung*, took the occasion of the Deutsche Bank Prize in Financial Economics to launch a series of articles about important economic researchers and their theories – and, by the way, it started with our laureate today.

This series of articles fully corresponded with the spirit of the Deutsche Bank Prize. In the pursuit of its aim to stimulate an international dialogue between researchers and practitioners, between central bankers and the financial services industry, I am confident the Center for Financial Studies and the jury could not have made a better decision than to select you, Professor Woodford.

Professor Woodford,

On behalf of the Group Executive Committee of Deutsche Bank and everyone here at Villa Sander today, I am very honored to be able to congratulate you as the winner of the Deutsche Bank Prize in Financial Economics 2007.

Thank you for being with us today.

Josef Ackermann, Michael Woodford

Volker Wieland

# OPENING SPEECHES AT THE SCIENTIFIC SYMPOSIUM

**Volker Wieland (Goethe University Frankfurt and CFS)**

Dear Michael and Argia,
Governor Mishkin, Mr. Lamberti,
President Issing,
Ladies and Gentlemen,

I am very happy to welcome you on behalf of the Center for Financial Studies at Goethe University to this symposium in honor of the recipient of the Deutsche Bank Prize in Financial Economics 2007. This year marks the second time the prize is awarded.

This prize, established by Goethe University and the Center for Financial Studies, aims to honor an internationally renowned researcher who has excelled through influential contributions to research in the fields of finance and money and macroeconomics, and whose work has led to practice – and policy-relevant results.

It is sponsored by the Stiftungsfonds Deutsche Bank im Stifterverband für die Deutsche Wissenschaft and carries a cash award of € 50,000, one of the highest in the field. In my view, Deutsche Bank has set a great example of corporate citizenship by endowing this scientific prize; which includes all costs associated with the nomination and selection process, the symposium and award ceremony.

As it is proper for such a major scientific award the responsibility lies with an independent institution, the CFS, and all matters regarding the nomination and selection process were decided by an independent prize jury of international experts. I had the pleasure to serve as Chairman.

In 2005 the prize was given to Eugene Fama for "developing and investigating the concept of market efficiency – a cornerstone in the area of finance."

As you certainly all know by now, this year's worthy recipient of the Deutsche Bank Prize is Professor Michael Woodford from Columbia University. Congratulations Mike!

Michael Woodford receives this prize for his fundamental contributions to "the theory and practical analysis of monetary policy." He has developed the so-called New-Keynesian theory of monetary economics that holds widespread appeal to academic researchers owing to its rigorous microeconomic foundations. And he has proved the immense practical value of this theory by analyzing the central role played by expectations and communication in the implementation of monetary policy.

Michael is joined here by his wife Argia Sbordone, herself an economist at the New York Fed who has contributed importantly to the empirical validation of the New-Keynesian approach.

Let me add a few more words regarding the illustrious group of speakers at this afternoon's symposium. The first session is led off by Professor Bennett T. McCallum from Carnegie-Mellon University. Ben is himself a leading authority in monetary economics. He will tell us more about Michael's achievements from the perspective of a grand master of the trade. He will be joined by Professor Jordi Galí, formerly also a professor at Columbia University, but now from Universitat Pompeu Fabra in Barcelona. Jordi is one of our very best European economists and has also been a key developer of New-Keynesian policy analysis.

We are particularly pleased that the keynote speech will be given by Governor Mishkin from the Federal Reserve, actually a Professor on leave from Columbia University. Governor Mishkin was crucial in pulling Michael into research on the practical aspects of monetary policy. As Research Director at the New York Fed he asked Michael to serve as the Bank's consultant.

We will further discuss the links between New-Keynesian theory and policy practice with Lucrezia Reichlin, Research Director at the European Central Bank and a jury member. She will show us how such models can be incorporated in the central bank policy process. Lucrezia is an expert econometrician and Professor on leave from Free University of Brussels. I will then discuss the role of money in monetary policy from the perspective of the New-Keynesian model.

We will close with a tremendous panel of experts on the theory and practice of monetary policy, starting with the prize winner himself. The panel includes Norbert Walter, Chief Economist of Deutsche Bank and a jury member as well as Professor Stefan Gerlach, formerly from the BIS and Chief Economist of the Hong Kong Monetary Authority, but since last month Professor at the University Frankfurt. It also includes Patrick Lane, Finance Editor of *The Economist* and jury member, and last but by no means least, Professor Otmar Issing, CFS President, former ECB Chief Economist and a member of the jury.

In closing, I am sure you agree with me that Deutsche Bank should be complimented for their very generous support of this endeavor. It is my privilege to welcome Hermann-Josef Lamberti, Member of the Management Board and Chief Operation Officer of Deutsche Bank AG, who will now speak to us.

Hermann-Josef Lamberti

**Hermann-Josef Lamberti (Deutsche Bank AG)**

Dear Professor Woodford,
dear Professor Wieland,
Ladies and Gentlemen,

It is a great pleasure for me to welcome you all in Frankfurt today. First of all, I would like to thank Professor Michael Woodford for accepting the Deutsche Bank Prize in Financial Economics 2007 that will be awarded to him at a ceremony later on. And I would like to thank him for joining this symposium on the "Theory and Practice of Monetary Policy Today". I am truly pleased that the second Deutsche Bank Prize in Financial Economics serves again as an occasion for a scientific symposium: An event that brings together first-rate experts of finance from academia and the corporate world.

Special thanks also go to Professor Volker Wieland for organizing today's symposium and for chairing the jury that has elected Professor Woodford for the Deutsche Bank Prize. And a special thank you also to the other members of the jury: Professor Otmar Issing from Frankfurt, Professor Lucrezia Reichlin from the ECB, Professor Lars Svensson from Princeton University, Professor Günter Franke from Konstanz University, Professor Jan Krahnen from the Center for Financial Studies (CFS), Professor Michael Haliassos and Professor Reinhard H. Schmidt from Frankfurt University, Patrick Lane from *The Economist* and Professor Norbert Walter from Deutsche Bank Group.

This independent jury has elected a worthy winner in a field of particular interest also to Deutsche Bank. Most of us in the financial sector have become so used to an environment of low and stable inflation rates, accompanied by an ever faster innovation in capital markets that we sometimes take monetary policy for granted – but it is not! How important is money? One of Michael Woodford's key questions has just recently shown its bite as financial institutions have struggled to find short-term liquidity in anxious markets. The theoretical discussion has to continue; changes in the real economy and in financial markets have to be evaluated; and the frameworks and strategies for monetary policy have to be re-assessed.

The contributions of Michael Woodford to the debate on monetary policy have been impressive. Over the past years these contributions have become increasingly visible to wider audience. His 2003 book *Interest and Prices* and his contributions to the discussion about Japan's deflation have been noticed outside academic and central bank circles. But the visibility of his models reached a new high in November 2006, when he spoke at the 4th ECB Central Banking Conference here in Frankfurt on "How important is money in the conduct of monetary policy?" His conclusions caused a considerable amount of controversy and this symposium is expected to focus on these controversies as well.

I am proud that Deutsche Bank has the opportunity to support the discussion on these important issues by sponsoring the Prize in Financial Economics. It is a discussion that has to happen at an international level – therefore I am pleased that so many participants at this symposium come from outside of Europe.

Economic discussion today has to be broad and diverse. It depends on criticism. But hasn't this always been the case? John Maynard Keynes wrote in his famous preface to the *General Theory* on December 1935: "It is astonishing what foolish things one can temporarily believe if one thinks too long alone, particularly in economics, where it is often impossible to bring one's ideas to a conclusive test either formal or experimental."

I am also excited that this important discussion is taking place in Frankfurt, where Deutsche Bank's global headquarter is located. Deutsche Bank, ECB and the many other banks, mutual funds, consulting and technology companies play an active part in making Frankfurt a cluster on financial market excellence. To this end, we need the best and brightest here – even if only temporarily, as is the case for some of you at this symposium. Attracting skills and fostering international diversity will be the most important factor for global competitiveness. Thus clustering and networking is so important.

The first Deutsche Bank Prize, awarded to Eugene Fama in 2005, demonstrated that the prize and the symposium were able to generate new perspectives and creative ideas. Eugene Fama emphasized the dependency of market efficiency on information available. The Symposium gave new impulses to the discussion and Eugene Fama with his charismatic personality was an inspiring role-model for younger people!

The first Deutsche Bank Prize had an impact here in Germany well beyond the day when the prize was awarded. To raise awareness to economic research, one of the leading newspapers in Germany, the *Frankfurter Allgemeine Zeitung*, took the opportunity of the Deutsche Bank Prize to start a serial about important economic researchers and their theories: It started, not a surprise, with our today's laureate, Michael Woodford!

This serial complies fully with the spirit of the Deutsche Bank Prize and with other Corporate Social Responsibility (CSR) activities of Deutsche Bank: Acting responsibly to shareholders, clients, employees and society as a whole in our business decisions and in raising awareness or support to important fields of business, markets, research or even culture and civil society. CSR is more than just money – it is about people and ideas – ideas which shape the views of the future.

The Prize in Financial Economics can be seen as a platform for further discussion — and for networking. The rapid change in financial markets demands well-functioning networks in order to recognize new developments and to examine them in terms of opportunities and risks. We are convinced that we need a wider international understanding of new developments in financial markets, for students and professors, for experts and executives in the industry and politics and for the public.

These networks are people-driven and require professional and personal relationships at different levels. I am sure that the high level participants on the panels and in the auditorium will make for inspiring discussions at today's symposium and for good networking! I wish you all a great day. Thank you!

Otmar Issing, Hermann-Josef Lamberti

# SUMMARY OF THE SCIENTIFIC SYMPOSIUM "THE THEORY AND PRACTICE OF MONETARY POLICY TODAY"

Celia Wieland (wieland EconConsult)

The Deutsche Bank Prize in Financial Economics is the most highly endowed international award given for outstanding academic achievements in the fields of money and finance with a practice and policy relevant orientation. It was established in 2005 by the Center for Financial Studies, in cooperation with Frankfurt University. The prize is sponsored by the Deutsche Bank Donation Fund and carries a cash award of € 50,000. It is awarded every two years.

The Deutsche Bank Prize for 2007 was awarded to Michael Woodford, Professor of Political Economy at Columbia University. Woodford received the prize in recognition of his fundamental contributions to the theory and practical analysis of monetary policy. According to the international prize jury, Woodford's research has led to a theory of monetary macroeconomics that holds widespread appeal for many researchers owing to its rigorous microeconomic foundations. The jury also praised the high practical value of Woodford's theories, based on which he analyzes the central role played by expectations and communication in the implementation of monetary policy.

Michael Woodford

An international scientific symposium headlined "The Theory and Practice of Monetary Policy Today" was organized for the occasion of the prize award ceremony in Frankfurt on 4 October 2007. 11 distinguished speakers, together with more than 200 international participants from academia, central banks, private institutions and banks, reviewed and debated the hypotheses, findings and policy implications of Woodford's research.

Hermann-Josef Lamberti

In his welcome address, the symposium organizer and chairman of the prize jury, Volker Wieland (Goethe University Frankfurt and CFS), congratulated Michael Woodford and stressed his important contributions to the development of the New-Keynesian theory of monetary economics, as well as the "immense practical value of this theory for analyzing the central role played by market expectations and central bank communication in the implementation of policy decisions."

Hermann-Josef Lamberti (Deutsche Bank AG), representing the sponsor of the award and event, complimented the independent jury for electing a very worthy prize winner. He emphasized the practical significance of Woodford's field of study and noted that financial markets have become so accustomed to an environment of low and stable inflation rates that the monetary policy that creates this environment is easily taken for granted. Lamberti asked "How important is money?" and pointed out that "one of Michael Woodford's key questions has just recently shown its bite as financial institutions have struggled to find short-term liquidity in anxious markets." He urged researchers to: Continue the theoretical discussion; evaluate changes in the real economy and in financial markets; and reassess the frameworks and

strategies for monetary policy. Deutsche Bank envisions the Prize in Financial Economics as a platform for furthering discussion, international networking and the promotion of a deeper understanding of monetary and financial developments.

Bennett T. McCallum

## The New-Keynesian Approach to Understanding the Economy

The first paper elucidating the New-Keynesian approach to monetary economics was presented by Bennett T. McCallum (Carnegie Mellon University), who is himself an eminent monetary theorist and academic. On

Woodford's influential monograph *Interest and Prices*, McCallum commented that it drastically diminishes the role of money in monetary policy analysis, but nevertheless, is "the most important treatise on monetary economics in over 50 years; it seems likely to go down in intellectual history as one of the handful of great books on this topic." The monograph develops the so-called "New-Keynesian" model that stands at the center of mainstream macroeconomic analysis today. McCallum noted that Woodford's analysis combines theoretical rigor, concern for empirical veracity, and respect for actual central bank practice to an extent that represents an enormous improvement over the situation of 25 years ago.

McCallum took issue with the common use of the term "New-Keynesian" as a description of the new mainstream approach. Rather, he said, "it has as much reason to be called 'New-Neoclassical Synthesis' as it was by Marvin Goodfriend and Robert King in 1997. In fact, in some important aspects the approach is actually closer to that of the 'monetarists' of the 1960-70's than the 'Keynesians' who they battled with." McCallum proceeded to present the key ingredients of the model, the so-called "New-Keynesian Phillips and IS curves" that, contrary to past Keynesian approaches, assign a primary role to the forward-looking expectations of market participants. He referred to the many useful extensions worked out in Woodford's monograph that help in fitting this model to empirical data and in linking macroeconomic outcomes and policy objectives to economic welfare considerations.

Jordi Galí (Universitat Pompeu Fabra), who is also an important contributor to the development of monetary policy analysis in the New-Keynesian framework, presented the second paper in this session. He described several of the insights and lessons gained from using this approach:

Jordi Galí

• Regarding the benefits of price stability, Galí explained how inflation serves as an indicator of an inefficient level of economic activity when prices are rigid. According to the simplest version of the New-Keynesian Phillips curve, deviations of output from the level that would be realized with fully flexible prices lead to inflation. Galí qualified this finding by pointing towards some arguments for a small, but positive rate of average inflation and the existence of short-run trade-offs between output and inflation stabilization. These qualifications suggest that the target rate for inflation should be achieved over the medium-run.

• Regarding the role of market expectations, Galí explained the drawbacks of a purely discretionary monetary policy. Instead, he advised incorporating commitment, i.e. rule-like, predictable behavior, in the practical design of policy so as to improve output-inflation trade-offs.

• Galí presented some of his own research, highlighting the importance of proper identification of the "natural" levels of output and interest rates as policy benchmarks.

In particular, he showed that the traditional approach for estimating output gaps (that is, deviations of output from its potential or natural level) implies rather different estimates from those derived on the basis of the New-Keynesian model. Thus, policy approaches using such traditional output gaps would perform badly in this model.

Galí concluded that the New-Keynesian approach represented a flexible tool that had delivered novel insights and proved useful in organizing macroeconomic analysis.

Frederic Mishkin

### Keynote Speech: Will Monetary Policy Become More of a Science?

Governor Frederic S. Mishkin (Board of Governors of the Federal Reserve System), a former colleague of Michael Woodford at Columbia University, shared his views on the usefulness of the science of monetary policy for policy practice with the Frankfurt audience, thus providing the perspective of an influential U.S. policymaker. According to Mishkin, the science of monetary policy is a set of principles derived from rigorous theory and empirical research that has helped produce greatly improved macroeconomic outcomes over the last 30 years. He identified these improvements in the form of lower inflation along with lower volatility of inflation and output. In particular, he provided a list of scientific discoveries of great importance for policy which are summarized above as Mishkin's 'TOP 9 Advances in the Science of Monetary Policy.'

## Mishkin's Top 9 Advances in the Science of Monetary Policy

1. *Inflation, as explained by the late Milton Friedman, is always and everywhere a monetary phenomenon and, therefore, under the control of central bank policy.*

2. *Price stability improves economic welfare because it increases the level of resources productively employed in the economy.*

3. *There is no long-run trade-off between unemployment and inflation, as demonstrated by Nobel Prize winners Milton Friedman and Edmund Phelps. In other words, central banks are not able to lower unemployment permanently by running up inflation.*

4. *Market expectations play a key role in the transmission of monetary policy to the economy, as shown by Michael Woodford's contributions.*

5. *The Taylor principle, named after John B. Taylor, emphasizes that central banks' interest rate policy needs to respond to fluctuations of inflation (or inflation expectations) by more than one for one, in order to guarantee price stability in the long-run.*

6. *The time-inconsistency problem. As shown by Nobel Prize winners Finn Kydland and Edward Prescott, discretionary policy leads to poor outcomes. Unfortunately, however, without institutions that provide a form of commitment, monetary policymakers will find themselves unable to consistently follow an optimal policy over time.*

7. *Central bank independence, therefore, represents a key element of successful institutional design.*

8. *Central banks need to commit to a nominal anchor.*

9. *Financial frictions and financial instability play an important role in the business cycle.*

Furthermore, Mishkin discussed several useful developments in the applied science of monetary policy linked, in particular, to the application of algorithmic methods and the development of econometric models used for the evaluation of alternative monetary policy strategies.

Mishkin acknowledged that despite all these scientific advances, there are good reasons why "art" or judgment will always be needed in monetary policy. Models simply cannot make use of all potentially valuable information. Yet, judgments must be guided by science. He concluded by pointing out a number of important avenues for further research, such as: (i) Building models with more sectors and better explanations of sluggish adjustment in nominal variables; (ii) modeling the heterogeneity of households and firms; (iii) including financial frictions in macroeconometric models; (iv) allowing for deviations from fully rational behavior by households and firms; (v) incorporating the learning behavior of economic decision makers; and (vi) further developing methods for evaluating the robustness of different monetary policy strategies under uncertainty about the proper model for the economy.

The papers in the next sections presented new research in two of these areas, namely how to combine judgment with model-based information in forecasting and how to render monetary policy more robust by cross-checking.

---

## The New-Keynesian Approach to Forecasting and Monetary Policy Design

---

Lucrezia Reichlin, Director General of Research at the European Central Bank, presented a paper that investigates how to incorporate conjunctural analysis in structural models of the New-Keynesian provenance. Reichlin emphasized the significance of

Jan Pieter Krahnen, Lucrezia Reichlin, Volker Wieland

Woodford's first attempts at estimating small scale New-Keynesian models together with Julio Rotemberg in 1997. Since then, larger and richer models of this type have been developed and are now used routinely in the forecasting exercises of many central banks. In her presentation, Reichlin explained how to combine such models with conjunctural analysis. In doing so, her objective is to improve forecasting and to use models to interpret conjunctural news.

Traditionally, the basic goal of conjunctural analysis has been to exploit early releases to judge the current state of the economy, in particular current quarter GDP. Qualitative judgment is typically combined with simple small-scale models sometimes termed "bridge equations". These equations provide a bridge between the information contained in one or a few key monthly indicators and the quarterly growth rate of GDP, when measurements on the latter are not yet available.

The methodological advances presented by Reichlin help improve forecasting in real time by
• using a large number of data series,
• updating now-casts and measures of their accuracy in accordance with the real time calendar of data releases, and
• "bridging" monthly data releases with the now-cast of quarterly GDP.

Such forecasting approaches have been implemented at the ECB, the Federal Reserve Board and the central banks of New Zealand and Norway. Reichlin concluded that quantitative New-Keynesian models that have become a regular element of the forecasting process can be complemented with reduced form models developed to interpret data flow in real time in order to improve forecasting performance and interpret shocks in real time.

Volker Wieland, Lucrezia Reichlin

The paper by Volker Wieland (Goethe University Frankfurt and CFS) investigates the robustness of monetary policy under uncertainty. Wieland, who praised Michael Woodford for his tremendous contributions to monetary theory and practice, suggested honoring Woodford also by debating one of his more controversial propositions. The award of the Deutsche Bank Prize 2007 to Michael Woodford had triggered substantial press and media interest in Germany in the run-up to the symposium due to Woodford's outspoken criticism of the ECB's two-pillar strategy, in particular, the prominent role of money in this strategy.

Wieland quoted Nobel Prize winner Robert Lucas who wrote in 2007 that "events since 1999 have not tested the importance of the (ECB's) second, monetary pillar ... I am concerned that this encouraging but brief period of success will foster the opinion, already widely held, that the monetary pillar is superfluous, and lead monetary policy analysis back to the kind of muddled eclecticism that brought us the 1970s inflation." Lucas noted the increasing reliance of central bank research on New-Keynesian modeling and questioned whether this approach was able to satisfactorily explain the relation between trend money growth and inflation. Lucas concluded that "this remains an unresolved issue on the frontier of macroeconomic theory. Until it is resolved, monetary information should continue to be used as a kind of add-on or cross-check, just as it is in the ECB policy formulation today."

Wieland's paper, written jointly with CFS fellow Günter Beck, uses the New-Keynesian model to address the concerns expressed by Robert Lucas. Money is present in this model but does not play a causal role in inflation determination once the effect of a central bank's interest rate policy on output and that of output on inflation is taken into account. The paper allows for imperfect knowledge and persistent central bank misperceptions regarding the natural rates of interest and output. These misperceptions are shown to cause sustained policy mistakes and trends in money and inflation like those pointed out by Lucas.

Wieland then presented a strategy that normally follows optimal decisions based on the New-Keynesian model (recognizing that central banks act under discretion), but is combined with cross-checking against long-run money growth. He demonstrated that such a strategy would improve inflation control in the case of persistent central bank misperceptions. "The policy rule with cross-checking ensures that sustained deviations of money growth and inflation from target due to policy mistakes are eventually corrected," according to Wieland. For example, such a correction occurs even when model-based inflation forecasts indicate that demand is sufficiently weak to return

inflation on track. Cross-checking is designed as a statistical test that triggers policy adjustments only in the event of sustained deviations. If the central bank's model estimates are correct, this strategy reaps the benefits of policy design in the New-Keynesian model, but if they are persistently mistaken, cross-checking improves inflation control and renders the policy strategy more robust.

## Expert Panel: The Theory and Practice of Monetary Policy Today – Successes, Failures and Open Questions

The symposium concluded with a panel of academic, centralbank and market experts, starting with the prize winner. Michael Woodford (Columbia University) noted that he agreed with Governor Mishkin's statement that inflation is always a monetary phenomenon but suggested that this statement is not always understood the same way.

According to Woodford, modern theory makes an important proposition by stating that inflation is almost entirely a consequence of central bank policies. In the models he uses, the inflation trend as well as shorter run fluctuations of inflation are critically determined by the actions and commitments of central banks. Based on these models, however, the proposition that inflation is a monetary phenomenon does

not have much to do with historical correlations between inflation and particular measures of the money supply. Nor is the money demand equation connecting the money supply and the general price level necessarily a key relationship in his model of the effects of monetary policy on inflation and output. Woodford, therefore, restated the principle of inflation being a monetary phenomenon as follows: The economic principle involved is the one according to which real factors in the economy determine at what equilibrium relative prices of goods and services are in the economy or what they will be once wages and prices have adjusted, but cannot determine what the absolute monetary level of the price of anything should be. Rather, it is only monetary policy commitments that can determine the latter.

Woodford then referred to the remarks of Robert Lucas quoted by Volker Wieland. Regarding the question on money growth and inflation trends, Woodford cited a paper he had written. This paper shows that inflation trends in the New-Keynesian models may be determined by the inflation target of the central bank without any relation to what is happening to the money supply. Woodford, however, acknowledged that the question of guarding against making mistakes because of inaccurate measurements of the economy that is addressed in Wieland's paper is a very important one. Woodford suggested the question of policy under uncertainty and cross-checking is an interesting topic for further research. However, Woodford expressed skepticism on whether monetary cross-checking constitutes the best approach to guarding against the kind of policy mistakes analyzed by Wieland, and suggested to use past inflation.

Finally, Woodford expressed support for the list of important research topics presented by Governor Mishkin. In particular, Woodford emphasized the need for developing a more satisfactory model of the financial sector and the

Chair: Michael Binder (CFS and Frankfurt Univer...)

Speakers: Michael Woodford (Columbia University)
Norbert Walter (Deutsche Bank AG)
Stefan Gerlach (Frankfurt University)
Patrick Lane (The Economist)
Otmar Issing (CFS and Frankfurt University)

Michael Binder, Michael Woodford, Norbert Walter, Stefan Gerlach, Patrick Lane, Otmar Issing

effects of financial frictions, and for investigating the robustness of monetary policy to alternative assumptions regarding expectations formation. Next, Norbert Walter (Deutsche Bank AG) provided the perspective of a practitioner who has been responsible for short- and medium-term forecasting for many years. According to Walter, the successes of monetary policy are very clear: Namely the anchoring of inflation expectations at such low levels in so many countries in a world of a fiat currency. This success has really come as a surprise. Walter doubted that many people would have predicted such an outcome 20 years ago. He urged central banks around the world to follow the example of those that had secured these achievements. He stated that central bank independence is an important reason for these achievements, but not the only one. Walter also speculated that the forces of globalization, in particular increased wage competition on a global level, made it easier for central banks to keep inflation low and anchor inflation expectations.

As to the failures of monetary policy, Walter said that obviously central banks have not been able to avoid asset price bubbles. Time and time again the world has seen financial crises due to market inefficiencies. Despite adamant support for flexible exchange rates, we have experienced

exchange rate changes that have been multiples of the differences in price and cost differentials between currency areas. Thus, there are a number of open questions regarding monetary strategy that need to be addressed. On money supply, Walter suggested that at times of massive financial innovation and disproportional increases in the demand for financial assets, the implications of these effects need to be

accounted for in terms of the ECB's monetary pillar. Walter underscored the uncertainties regarding concepts such as "natural" output or unemployment rates given the difficulties in measuring productivity and the effects of extensive off-shoring and trade in services.

Stefan Gerlach (Goethe University Frankfurt) elaborated on the achievements of monetary policy. In particular, he highlighted the important role of central bank independence and the successes in managing monetary policy as a technical undertaking relying on economic analysis and economists in central banks. He noted that research has contributed to central bank independence as well as improved our understanding of the transmission mechanism. As to open questions, Gerlach asked whether more transparency would always improve policy performance or whether there are limits to transparency. He mentioned the benefits that may be obtained by organizing decision-making by monetary policy committees rather than by individuals, and noted the importance of outsiders as external members of such committees. Regarding the inflation process itself, Gerlach considered the first generation of New-Keynesian Phillips curve models too simple and suggested a greater role for globalization. In Gerlach's judgment, inflation targeting strategies have been so successful simply due to the greater focus on inflation rather than the various technical features. Finally, he emphasized that the proper policy response to asset price inflation remains on important open question.

Patrick Lane (*The Economist*) also noted the success of monetary policy in achieving low and stable inflation. He considered it an enormous achievement given the state of many economies in the 1970s. But, one explanation could be just luck. Even Alan Greenspan speaks in his memoirs of having been to a certain extent lucky. What other elements may there be behind this success? First, there has been a remarkably successful move away from politics. Second, central banks have concentrated on a nominal anchor for fiat money. Third, the role of expectations has been recognized in monetary theory and practice. Fourth, it has been understood that it is key for central banks to keep their promises. Thus, a great deal has

Norbert Walter, Stefan Gerlach

changed in central bank communication in past years. Failures in policy are unlikely to be avoided because the world is uncertain. Studying the implications of such failures or misperceptions is certainly an important area for research. There are many open questions. For example, what prices should central banks aim to stabilize? How should central banks communicate with the market and the public? And given the turmoil of the past couple of months, what role should be given to the financial industry and credit in monetary policy analysis?

Patrick Lane, Otmar Issing

In conclusion, Otmar Issing, President of the Center for Financial Studies and former ECB Chief Economist, concentrated on the fundamental challenges the ECB faced when preparing for the start of monetary policy. As a new institution, one without a track record and responsible for a currency still to be born, the ECB had to overcome a lot of skepticism. But the ECB lived up to the challenge to anchor inflation expectations on a level consistent with its mandate and to maintain price stability, and has proved to be successful. The ECB achieved this by convincing markets and the public that it was determined to make the euro a stable currency and that it would be able to do so. By announcing its quantitative definition of price stability in the form of the two-pillar strategy, the ECB set an important milestone.

Communication, transparency and a clear commitment to the policy goal are the same principles that can be found at the core of Michael Woodford's book *Interest and Prices.* Thus, in this regard, Issing agreed with Woodford. He disagreed, however, on the role

of money. "In a world in which financial markets play an ever increasing role, can we really rely on models that do not include a fully developed financial sector?" Issing asked. While many have criticized the ECB's strategy, in particular the role of money and cross-checking, Issing said he considered it the best available approach. In his view, ignoring money and credit is not the solution.

Issing concluded that central banks have probably never been so successful in achieving low inflation. The big failures have occurred when central banks have tried to fine tune the economy and ignored money. Furthermore, some open questions still remain, which is encouraging for younger and older economists alike.

Josef Ackermann, Michael Woodford, Volker Wieland

# THE THEORY AND PRACTICE OF MONETARY POLICY TODAY – SUCCESSES, FAILURES AND OPEN QUESTIONS

Norbert Walter

**Norbert Walter (Deutsche Bank AG)**

## Introduction

Monetary policy is and remains a challenging policy area – even if the calm monetary environment at the moment may be taken to suggest that things are running according to plan. Monetary history shows us that just when we start to believe we had arrived at a stable routine of keeping inflation at bay, new issues for monetary policy arise. Monetary policy is all about expectations, and "expectations" means past developments plus an error term. It is the error term that all of us are most interested in

unexpected risks, our failure to assess future developments. And this is why discussions between academics and market practitioners, like on this panel, are so important. Let me address four key issues that I believe will occupy us in the future:

## The Ostensible Success of Monetary Policy

If I was to make an executive summary of monetary policy in Europe and the U.S. in the past years, I would underscore its ostensible achievements. At least broadly speaking. Importantly, central bankers have succeeded in anchoring inflation expectations at historically low levels in a large number of countries. This is all the more remarkable considering the many hurdles fiat money regimes need to overcome on the way. The temptation of printing money to pursue short-term political ends is the central difficulty for such systems. There is little doubt that making central banks as independent from electoral politics as possible in democratic societies has become widely accepted and has greatly contributed to the recent stability.

Today, this seems like an obvious observation, but it is worthwhile recalling that only two or three decades ago, this was a very contended issue.

The establishment of the European Central Bank and its integration into the E.U.'s legal order as an independent authority so far marks the culmination in the long march of practically implementing a theoretical postulate that can be traced back to David Ricardo and has been advocated by monetary economists in varying forms ever since. I am hopeful and confident that this approach will prevail – to the benefit of our societies.

## The Importance of the Economic Environment

As essential as institutional arrangements are as a precondition for stable monetary policy, the economic environment in which monetary policy is conducted remains an important co-determinant for its success or failure.

The current state of the global economy is a suitable example. The era of globalization, the opening-up of markets and increasing competition has been an easy time for central banks to keep inflation low and anchor expectations. The recent years have been a period when a lot of additional relatively skilled labour entered the market. As a result, cost pressures have been less pronounced than in earlier periods. Of course, this benign environment also goes back to groundbreaking political initiatives. In particular, I am thinking of the creation of the single market in the E.U., which has proven an indispensable condition for stable growth in Europe, and therefore for monetary union. Another example is the increasingly free flow of goods, services, and capital around the world, which has been facilitated by an unprecedented liberalization of markets between the key economies in this world, including the U.S., the E.U., and many key emerging markets. The line of causation may not be a direct one, but dismantling artificial market barriers and promoting free and efficient markets are for all we know key elements of a stable macroeconomic environment, and policymakers are well-advised to maintain and actually reinforce their commitment to open markets. This prominently includes policy initiatives such as the Doha trade round, the liberalization of investment flows, or the global convergence of financial market regulation.

## Global Risks to Monetary Stability

All these factors cannot belie the fact that substantial risks to monetary stability remain. In fair weather, most systems tend to function, some better than others. What we need to ensure, of course, is that our monetary order functions as smoothly once market events or external effects rock the boat. Let me be explicit on this point: This is no fear-mongering. Our economies are vulnerable to a variety of shocks, the sources of which may range from geopolitics, to market inefficiencies, to natural catastrophes. Some of them are very real, and monetary policy must need to be prepared. On the economic side, they include:

• Easy money in the first years of this decade, and its implications for price stability and financial asset prices,

• the global imbalances in current accounts,

• the huge swings of the major global currencies the Euro and the U.S.-Dollar,

• and the danger of irrational exuberance on financial markets, as exemplified by the sub-prime lending market in the U.S. and its recent collapse.

All of these operational threats are latent, and they confront our monetary system at a time when many conceptual issues about optimizing monetary regimes remain unresolved. This, in my view, makes the current situation even more fragile than it appears to be. Let me address just a handful of key conceptual issues:

- Most importantly, the question of optimal monetary targeting is still in the air. Money supply and inflation targeting are two paradigms that are being discussed with rigor. Michael Woodford's question "How important is money in the conduct of monetary policy?" points precisely at this issue, and his research provides important clarification.

- Closely related to monetary targeting is the topic of asset prices and how to include them in our monetary models. In other words: What is the appropriate way of valuing equity, real estate, and other financial markets which have seen astonishing growth rates over the past years. And, with a view to monetary policy, whether and how these asset price changes should be included in our measurement of overall inflation in our economies?

- Finally, we need to obtain a better understanding of the impact of financial innovation on the monetary condition. Key questions include how the rise e.g. of non-bank financial institutions that we have witnessed over the past years affects monetary transmissions. Overall, the different developments in technology in the international arena, with their impact on productivity, often do not reflect the true development of productivity but just its measurement according to different concepts in national income accounts. In addition, there are a number of changes in the institutional set-up for factors like the work force, particularly in aging societies, the change in participation rates through changes of attitudes, surprising migration,

the shadow economy, guest workers. These dynamics make it very difficult to pursue monetary policy in line with trend growth, since the latter is difficult to assess and may vary considerable over the medium term.

Norbert Walter, Stefan Gerlach

## National Monetary Approaches in a Globalized Economy?

Finally, let me address a topic that I believe represents one of the most challenging policy issues of our time, namely the role of nationally-centred policy approaches in an increasingly globalized economy. It occurs to me that we should be interested in a much more global view and approach to monetary policy than we seem to be at the moment. National perspectives still dominate our policies, and I am not sure whether the challenges that we may expect in the future may not require a much more international and cooperative strategy. Let me provide two examples:

- For one thing, it appears odd to me that we continue to look at national statistics in order to truly evaluate monetary policy in a world that has extended beyond national borders. Instead, markets are global, and that even goes to a considerable extent for labour markets, parts of which today are characterized by outsourcing, nearshoring, and a busy flow of labour across borders. Against this background, we may wish to revisit our understanding of the NAIRU as a purely national concept.

• Similarly, I believe that we can benefit from getting a much better understanding of the role of national monetary policies and their interrelation with exchange rate policies, particularly in a situation when more and more often shocks to our financial markets and shocks to our mature economies are symmetric. Some monetary economists seem to consider that the foreign exchange rate is a tool for national monetary policy. This perception violates fundamentally the logical fact that the exchange rate is the price of two currencies and that if more and more often shocks are symmetric, a fixed exchange-rate regime as a national concept has the effect of a beggar-thy-neighbour policy. Given the global monetary and exchange rate environment in the age of global imbalances, it occurs to me that this latter perspective is particularly valid and deserves greater attention.

• Finally, there seems to be merit in great conceptual work on better institutional cooperation among monetary and exchange rate authorities. Certainly, the Bank for International Settlements, the Financial Stability Forum, and the International Monetary Fund provide important fora for exchanging information and views on monetary policy, stability, and macro-prudential supervision. The system, however, remains highly fragmented, and it can be legitimately wondered how well it would perform under conditions of stress at a regional or global scale. From my perspective, closer cooperation on monetary, exchange rate, and macro-prudential supervision is a worthwhile effort, and I think more work both in science and in practice is urgent.

## Conclusion

Monetary policy can legitimately look back on a number of key successes over the past years. But neither policymakers nor academic scholars – nor bank economists like me, for that matter – should get complacent about the smooth functioning of the global monetary system at the moment. The risks to the system are ample, and policymakers, market participants and scientists should always be prepared for the expected and the unexpected. Not separately, but together, of course. The closer the three groups cooperate, the more likely we are to succeed in making the monetary system more efficient, stable, and reliable.

Stefan Gerlach

**Stefan Gerlach (Goethe University Frankfurt)**

It is great privilege to participate in this session on "The Theory and Practice of Monetary Policy Today: Successes, Failures and Open Questions" and to celebrate Michael Woodford receiving the Deutsche Bank Prize in Financial Economics 2007.

Let me start by noting that monetary policy in the last twenty years has been very, if not staggeringly, successful. To my mind, this all came about as a consequence of the world wide move towards greater central bank independence that started in the 1990s. This shift was coupled with the introduction of monetary policy strategies that focused squarely on price stability and with a sharp increase in transparency. Being free to set interest rates to achieve an explicit objective for the rate of inflation, and with little ability to hide uncomfortable truths about their performance, central banks found themselves in an entirely new situation.

These changes brought a greater need for careful analysis of economic developments in general and inflation in particular. In response, central banks expanded and strengthened their economics and research departments: From the perspectives of monetary economists, the last two decades have been a boondoggle. Of course, some central banks, in particular the Federal Reserve, already had many highly trained economists on their staff, but other central banks – in particular those that had previously operated under fixed exchange rates with currency controls – were not always in this favorable position.

The growing importance of economic analysis in central banks in turn stimulated research about monetary policy in the academic sector, a development that Mike's work is an excellent illustration of. Furthermore, the shift toward greater central bank independence was itself a reaction to research that established that average inflation rates had been systematically lower in economies in which the central bank was more independent.

This flood of new research, which was conducted at universities and central banks, contributed enormously to our understanding of many important questions, such as the transmission mechanism of monetary policy, the role of expectations and their implications for the setting of policy, and the importance of transparency, to mention but a few. At the same time, great progress was made in the area of econometrics and model building, partially as a consequence of rapid developments in information technology. In sum, theoretical and empirical work on monetary policy has taken a huge step forward since the early 1990s and has played an important role in improving the conduct of monetary policy.

But not all problems have been solved. Let me raise a few questions which I think are still alive and well.

First, there is a strong presumption in the literature on monetary policy that more trans-parency is always better. Yet central banks systematically limit the amount of information they provide to the public. Most obviously, many have a purdah period, during which they do not comment on monetary policy, in the week(s) before policy meetings. If more information is always good and if agents learn to downplay irrelevant information, it is difficult to see the rationale for this practice. I suspect that the same factors that make central banks have purdah periods also play a role in explaining why they limit transparency at other times.

In any case, more work is needed on these issues.

A second area in which more work is required concerns monetary policy decision making rules. There is formal evidence that outsiders at the Bank of England's MPC vote systematically different from insiders, and that these differences have been stable since the committee was established more than a decade ago. I suspect that having outsiders involved in the setting of monetary policy is a good idea – it avoids group thinking as they have less time to be exposed to the central bank's internal views of the functioning of the economy – but up to date there is no formal evidence indicating that this is true.

Norbert Walter, Stefan Gerlach, Patrick Lane

Third, more work on understanding why inflation targeting has been such a successful policy strategy would be desirable. One view is that inflation targeting "works" because of all the paraphernalia that are typically associated with it: For instance, inflation reports, the development of forecasting models and new decision making procedures. The competing view is that what really matters is the greater focus on inflation in setting monetary policy that inflation targeting has brought. Needless to say, knowing the relative importance of these two factors is helpful in designing monetary policy frameworks.

Fourth and finally, we need to know better how to handle asset prices in inflation targeting regimes. One view, which I believe most central banks subscribe to, is that central banks should only respond to asset prices to the extent that they contain information about future inflation. The competing view is that monetary policy should react to asset prices over and beyond what they imply for inflation. One reason for this, it is argued, is that asset price booms are likely to end with a collapse that may take many years to occur, leading to macroeconomic weakness and inflation falling below the central bank's target or objective. According to this view, attaching weight to asset prices can help ensure that inflation is stable also over longer time horizons than the two or three years that central banks typically focus on when setting monetary policy. Whether that is true remains to be seen.

Mike has moved the profession a tremendous step forward by providing tight analysis of a number of monetary policy problems, and his work has been highly influential in and outside of central banks. But many other questions remain, and I am sure that in the coming years we will see many more papers of him on these important questions.

Patrick Lane

**Patrick Lane (The Economist)**

I would like to start by thanking Volker Wieland on two counts: First, for inviting me to participate in the committee to award the Deutsche Bank Prize; second, for inviting me to join this panel today at the symposium to honour such a distinguished prizewinner, Michael Woodford.

When I saw the topic for this panel discussion, my first thought was to draw up a grid with two columns and three rows. The columns would be headed "theory" and "practice" and the rows "successes", "failures" and "open questions". Entries could then be made in each of the six fields. But I decided not to. I saw I was speaking fourth, so there was a good chance that someone else would use the idea before me.

And there was a more respectable reason, which was that at least two of the lines on that grid seem to me to be blurred. Theory and practice presumably reinforce each other. The other blurred line is the one between failures and open questions. Presumably if there are failures in theory or policy, those merely raise more open questions to be pursued at a later day.

In matters of policy the theoretical and the practical reinforce one another. It can be counted a success, for example, that central banks are largely independent of politicians. The exact form of independence varies from place to place – and in some countries, such as the one I come from, could in principle be easily reversed. But is this a success of theory? Maybe, in the sense that we have theories that suggest why this might be a good idea. Is it a success of practice? Yes again, in that monetary policy seems to work better when run by independent technicians rather than politicians with an eye on the next election. But which counts for more? Practice, I would say, given the importance of institutional detail, but the theoretical arguments count too.

Theory informs practice and points out possible flaws in it, ideally before they happen. Practical problems tell you what the interesting lines of theoretical inquiry ought to be. So in the time available I will trot quickly through what seem to me to be the main successes, failures and open questions. Some will be theoretical, some practical: some a mixture of the two.

## Successes

The most obvious success of monetary policy in recent years can be seen by looking at inflation over the past 30 years. Simply, in the 1970s inflation was high and variable; these days, it is low and stable and expected to stay that way.

The reasons behind this success are more interesting. One candidate is luck. Alan Greenspan, in his memoirs, rather modestly suggests that he was pretty lucky, by stressing the role of globalization in reducing inflationary pressures. I can see that a positive supply shock will, other things equal, give a central bank the opportunity to hold down inflationary expectations, and even give it a window of opportunity to chance to reduce its inflation target. But as a long-run explanation, it won't do. Ultimately, globalization shifts only relative prices; it is monetary policy that counts.

I would list three elements here. One is the independence of central banks, already mentioned. It's remarkable that we now look across at the People's Bank of China and regard the fact that it is beneath the state council and has to report to it as a sort of antediluvian practice, whereas ten years ago the Bank of England was in a similar, subservient position.

It is remarkable that so many countries seem to have come to the conclusion that it seems to be better if you divorce the conduct of monetary policy from the pursuit of short-term political gain by politicians. The definition of course varies from place to place. The constitutional basis for it in the U.K., if you look at it in detail, is somewhat fragile. Nevertheless, it remains independent.

A second is the concentration on a nominal anchor for monetary policy – a means of bringing to a world of fiat money some of the stability that many thought had disappeared with the gold standard. Once, monetary aggregates were the favourite, but in many places that proved more successful in theory than in practice. Inflation itself is the favourite in many places – but the precise definition is an open question.

A third is the emphasis on expectations. That has certainly improved the theory: Compare the New-Keynesian Phillips curve with the old pre-Friedman-Phelps-Lucas version. It has improved practice too, largely through its influence on communications. When I became an economic journalist – less than 14 years ago – the Fed did not even deign to tell the markets that it had changed its target for the Fed Funds Rate. And on several Thursdays in the proof-reading room of *The Economist* we would scramble, just before the magazine was put to bed, to write a few lines beginning with the words "The Bundesbank surprised the markets". Those days are gone, but the best form of communication remains very much an open question.

## Failures

I do not want to dwell long on the failures. Like Stefan Gerlach, I think it would be slightly churlish to mention any. Some, in terms of policy as opposed to theory, are inevitable simply because the world is uncertain. The implications of those failures or misperceptions of central bank policy are obviously an important line of research.

## Open questions

The list of open questions is long and no doubt could occupy us for much more than the time allotted. I will mention only three. One is the measure of inflation that central banks should target: Should it be core, should it be a broader measure of consumer prices or should it include some assets as well? I know that Michael Woodford has set out an argument for focusing on the core – if I understand the argument correctly – because these are the stickiest prices: Targeting more flexible prices runs the risk of distorting allocative price signals.

I am not sure of the answer to this, although I would prefer broader measures to narrower ones. I do think that more attention will have to be paid to the treatment of housing in official inflation measures, at least in Europe. In Britain and the euro zone, these are not included at all in the HICP. Given the importance of housing in household budgets, this is a remarkable omission.

A second is the way in which central banks communicate with markets and the public. Lately a lot of attention has been devoted to the publication by a few central banks of their own forecasts of interest-rate paths and of inflation and output forecasts based on them rather than on market or constant rate forecasts. Why base your forecasts on something you do not believe?

This is a good question and the publication of forecast rate paths is an intriguing development. It will be interesting to see how far the practice spreads. I think that some objections to it are unconvincing. It has been argued, for example, that the rate forecast may be treated as a commitment by the markets. But central banks should be able to communicate the probabilistic nature of these forecasts. And looking at how often the New Zealanders, the pioneers, have changed their forecasts and how quickly and how far the Swedes, who joined the club this year, changed theirs this spring, it seems unlikely that the markets would treat a forecast as a promise. A better objection, to my mind, is the opposite: The forecasts have not been very accurate, and so do not contain all that much information, more than a couple of quarters ahead. Another good reason for doubt is the difficulty of getting a committee to agree on a forecast. When each quarterly step in the forecast is conditional on what is assumed to have gone before, the decision tree quickly gets complicated. The experience of the Sveriges Riskbank in this respect will be well worth watching.

However, the biggest open question, given the turmoil of the past couple of months, lies in the connection between macroeconomics and the financial world. There is a broader question here, I think: How far should monetary policy try to take into account developments in financial markets and industries? The upheavals we have seen in the past couple of months have their roots partly in such developments: Securitization meant a divorce between mortgage lenders and the ultimate bearer of risk; globalization meant that American subprime defaults caught out European banks and have pushed up market rates in both Britain and the euro zone.

You can look at these developments from different angles. One is via the work of Ben Bernanke and others on credit channels, financial accelerators and so forth. Another is from the monetary side: It seems at least conceivable that changes in the financial industry may make banks more willing to lend, given the official policy rate. That ought to show up in monetary statistics, which may provide valuable information. Whether it is valuable or not is an empirical question.

Otmar Issing

**Otmar Issing (Goethe University Frankfurt and CFS)**

I would like to join all in congratulating Michael Woodford for being awarded the Deutsche Bank Prize in Financial Economics. This is not his first award, and – although I am always sceptical on forecasts – I am sure not the last one. And we all agree – he deserves it. I am grateful for his focus on monetary policy in general and especially for his visits to the ECB which gave us the great opportunity to discuss relevant topics with him. His contribution to modern macroeconomics is outstanding. Ben McCallum, Jordi Galí and all the others have demonstrated his great influence. I remember when I first met Michael at the Bundesbank. Listening to him made you aware what a clear mind was presenting his position with strong arguments. Ben McCallum in his intellectual honesty has made the point: It is difficult to win

the argument with Michael Woodford – even if you don't like the result. But like Ben I will never give up on issues where I fundamentally disagree which is on the role of money. Since we have met often at different places in the world and I had the privilege to learn from him in so many discussions especially during my time at the ECB.

Using the title of this panel I will concentrate on a success story and you will not be surprised. From the first day on in the ECB preparing for the start of monetary policy the key question was: As a new institution, without a track record, responsible for a currency still to be born – how could we overcome the scepticism prevailing in financial markets and with the general public?

To cut it short: The fundamental challenge was to anchor inflation expectations on a level consistent with our mandate which is to maintain price stability.

Today there is no doubt: The ECB was successful, inflation expectations didn't move after the disappearance of stable currencies like the DM. Instead, inflation expectations for the euro were well anchored.

How did we achieve that?

With the announcement of our two-pillar-strategy in October 1998 i.e. 10 weeks before the start of our monetary policy we convinced markets, the public – though not all academics – in a transparent way that we would not only be determined to make the euro a stable currency, but that we would also be able to achieve that. The announcement of a quantitative definition of price stability was an important element in this announcement.

Communication, transparency and a clear commitment to our goal were the elements which are also at the core of Michael Woodford's famous book *Interest and Prices*. There is no disagreement on that between us and – you will not be surprised – I like Mike's comments most when he praises the ECB's success. And, he has done so repeatedly. Public attention is mostly concentrated on critique – this gives a very biased view on Michael Woodford's position as to the ECB and its achievements.

However, before it gets boring, we also have continuing disagreements, the most fundamental one being that on the role of money – in a very broad sense. Following the title of this panel I would place it as a question: In a world in which financial markets play an ever increasing role can we really rely on models which do not include a fully developed financial sector?

Can we ignore money and credit as a driving force of macroeconomic developments – and not just dealing with this as endogenous variables?

Stefan Gerlach has raised the issue of the relation of monetary policy and asset prices. Here I just refer to important work at the BIS by C. Borio and his colleagues and at the ECB by F. Smets and colleagues.

Michael Woodford, Norbert Walter, Stefan Gerlach, Otmar Issing

You may criticize the ECB's strategy e.g. that the role of cross-checking is difficult to understand but, where is an alternative – a more convincing approach? Just ignoring money and credit cannot be the solution.

Finally, I couldn't agree more with Michael Woodford on the role of communication. However, guiding, anchoring expectations by communication has its limits. Therefore, I am sceptical on this suggestion of announcing an interest rate path by the Central Bank as presented in a number of publications – the latest one in the *Frankfurter Allgemeine Zeitung*.

**Let me just raise a few questions:**

• *How could we expect that markets always understand the conditionality of such an announcement?*

• *How can a central bank with a committee structure for decision making agree on an interest rate path? And how can communication cope with this structure?*

• *Is an inflation forecast an encompassing approach? What about asset prices and the time horizon of the forecast?*

Coming back to the title of this panel:

**Let me conclude with a few remarks:**

• *Central banks have probably never been so successful — inflation is low worldwide.*

• *The big failures occurred when central banks tried to fine tune the economy and ignored money.*

• *Open questions remain which is encouraging for all young — and older — economists.*

Notwithstanding Michael Woodford's publications the book on the state of the art of central banking is far from being closed. There is still a role for central bankers to study closely different approaches and make their choice.

Printing and Binding: Stürtz GmbH, Würzburg